An Introduction to
Irish Planning Law

An Introduction to
Irish Planning Law

Berna Grist
Barrister-at-Law
Chartered Town Planner

INSTITUTE OF PUBLIC
ADMINISTRATION

First published in 1999
by the Institute of Public Administration
57-61 Lansdowne Road
Dublin 4
Ireland.

www.ipa.ie

British Library Cataloguing in Publication Data
A catalogue record for this book is available from the British
Library.

ISBN 1 902448 27 8

Cover design by M & J Graphics Ltd.
Typeset by the Institute of Public Administration
Printed by Johnswood Press

TO THE MEMORY OF MY PARENTS
VIN AND ANN GRIST

CONTENTS

Preface

This book began as a section on the planning system which I was invited to contribute to a reader in local government studies some time ago. The lacuna between the eleven guidance leaflets issued by the Department of the Environment on various aspects of planning and the legal textbooks written by my learned colleagues has long been recognised and commented on by the participants in the planning process - those offering professional services such as architects, engineers and planning consultants, the officials of local authorities, elected public representatives and individuals or organisations wishing to exercise their statutory third party rights. Indeed, the lack of an introductory work on this topic was something I had frequently noted with regret in the course of preparing my lectures on administration and planning law for the students of the Master of Regional and Urban Planning degree programme at University College, Dublin. In attempting to answer this need, my contribution grew into a book, which sets out to present a complex and technical area of the law in a convenient format for those who are not themselves lawyers.

The current planning system came into operation just thirty-five years ago on 1 October 1964. In the intervening decades, the activities of planners and the issues with which they are faced have expanded and changed, principally in the areas of socio-economic development and environmental protection. However, the image and the reality can differ here. The general perception of planning encompasses matters dealt with under other legislative codes and the reader who wants an overall understanding of what is being achieved and what is yet to be addressed in this wider sense of planning will not find it sufficient to look merely at the nine Planning Acts and their associated twelve sets of Regulations. Accordingly, in the last three chapters, I have set out to cover the legal and administrative framework within which regional planning, urban renewal and other related areas are being approached.

As this book was going to print, the long promised Bill to revise and consolidate the Planning Acts was published. Some explanation is obviously needed to justify the decision not to delay publication of the book until the Bill is enacted.

This major proposal to reform the law relating to planning has been in preparation since mid-1997, when a comprehensive review of the planning code was initiated by the newly appointed Minister for the Environment and Local Government, Noel Dempsey, TD. The 1999 Planning Bill contains 245 sections and the constitutionality of its provisions relating to social and affordable housing is already being called into question. It was felt that this book would serve its purpose for all those who still have to make their way through the labyrinth that is the current planning system and who may have to do so for some time yet to come. The many participants in the planning process are being given a period to reflect and make observations on the Planning Bill and, as a solid comprehension of the present position is necessary to comment on future changes, I would hope this book will assist in the scrutiny of the system under review. The Institute of Public Administration, as publisher, is committed to an immediate Second Edition when the Bill becomes law.

A debt of gratitude is owed to the many persons who kindly assisted me with information and advice and by reading drafts of various chapters. While it is not possible to mention them all, I would particularly like to thank the following: Eoghan Brangan, Oonagh Buckley, Finian Matthews, Betty Moriarty, Mary Moylan and Feargal Ó Coigligh in the Department of the Environment and Local Government; Rachel MacRory in the Department of Arts, Heritage, Gaeltacht and the Islands; Frances Keegan in the Department of Tourism, Sport and Recreation; Peter Redmond in Dúchas; Terry Durney and Carmel Smith in the Dublin Docklands Development Authority; Willie Carroll in the Dublin Regional Authority; Paul Mullally in An Bord Pleanála; Leo Crehan and Paddy McLoughlin in Dublin Corporation; Brendan Morrissey in Fingal County Council; Terry Ó Niadh and Seamus Stokes in Kildare County Council; John Fry in the Department of Environmental Resource Management, UCD.

I must acknowledge the part played by my students, whose attentive questions have helped me identify the main issues which need to be addressed in coming to an understanding of the planning system. I am also grateful to Marguerite Curran and Deirdre Daly who typed the text and whose patience and courtesy never failed when faced with amendments and revisions.   Finally, my special thanks are due to my husband, Michael Kenny, for his encouragement and tolerance.

I have endeavoured to state the law as on 31 August 1999.

Berna Grist
University College, Dublin.
September, 1999.

CHAPTER 1

Introduction

Physical planning in Ireland formally commenced with the enactment of the 1934 Town and Regional Planning Act. Of course, from the mid nineteenth century onward, various pieces of legislation had allowed urban authorities to provide public open space[1] – a positive power to improve amenities in their area – and parts of the Public Health and Housing Acts created a rudimentary framework for control of development, but with the narrow objective of securing the health of the population. The 1934 Act introduced a coherent system of positive and regulatory planning based on the making by the planning authority of a planning scheme (the precursor of the development plan), which was to govern the carrying out of future development.

Town and Regional Planning Acts, 1934–39
However, in the 1930s neither the general public nor the politicians had much interest in planning[2], probably because of the lack of development pressures in a stagnant economy with widespread emigration. An amending Act in 1939 was intended to reduce the rigidity of the planning scheme procedure but there was no great enthusiasm for this new function and, as the 1934 and 1939 Acts were adoptive, few authorities passed the necessary resolution to give themselves planning powers. It has been calculated that, in 1952, only seventeen of the twenty-seven county councils had adopted the Planning Acts and, even in 1962, three counties still had not done so[3]. Their reluctance may have been not only a reflection of very limited development pressures but also a recognition that the planning scheme procedure was extremely complicated to operate.

Having adopted the Planning Acts, a planning authority had to prepare its planning scheme 'with all convenient speed'[4]. The amount and difficulty of the work involved

1

caused some authorities to abandon the attempt[5].   The
single planning scheme prepared, the 1957 Draft Dublin
Planning Scheme, was drawn up only after protracted
litigation by a building company[6] and, if the Corporation
had not completed a considerable amount of the
preparation prior to the action being initiated, the two or
three years allowed by the Court would not have been
adequate for its completion[7]. Having been adopted by the
Corporation, the Dublin Planning Scheme was submitted
for approval to the Minister and some 3,600 objections were
made against it. The Department of Local Government was
ill–equipped to deal with this hot potato and yet it was
essential to dispose of the scheme one way or the other[8]. In
1960, a planning expert, Charles Abrams, was invited to
Ireland from the UN at the Government's request and the
Irish planning system we know today has been derived from
his report and from the British Town and Country Planning
Act of 1947.   The 1934 and 1939 Town and Regional
Planning Acts were repealed[9] and no final decision ever had
to be taken on the Dublin Planning Scheme.

Administrative context

Planning is primarily a function or (to use the preferred
terminology of the 1990s) a service of local government.
The two–tier structure of the Irish local government system
was established by the 1898 Local Government (Ireland)
Act. Appendix IV contains a schedule of all local authorities
ranked according to status.

       The upper tier consists of the larger local authorities –
the county councils and the county borough corporations.
In 1898, a democratically elected body was established in
each of the existing thirty-three administrative counties[10].
Management of the financial and administrative business of
the county was entrusted to this council, which consisted of
a chairman and councillors. There were in existence at the
passing of the Act six borough corporations, which had
more extensive powers than the other urban authorities.
The 1898 Act provided that the mayors, aldermen and
burgesses of each of these borough corporations would
have the same powers and duties as a county council. They

were therefore created county borough corporations (CBCs) and, being administrative counties in themselves, were independent of the county in which they were geographically situated.

In 1898, the lower tier of local government consisted of the remaining five borough corporations, urban districts councils, town commissioners and rural district councils. The functions of the latter were taken over by the county councils in 1925. These lower tier elected bodies have responsibility for a reduced range of local government functions.

The 1898 Act vested considerable powers in the county councils and county borough corporations. As it also extended the franchise, a considerable measure of democracy came to the Irish countryside with dramatic suddenness and the county councils, in particular, became centres of nationalism[11]. However, these local authorities were not efficient, their members were prone to nepotism and susceptible to pressures of various kinds. The new ministers and their senior civil servants took a very strict line with the local authorities, a number of which were dissolved during the 1920s for failing to discharge their duties. They were replaced by salaried commissioners, who were efficient, had administrative expertise and displayed complete impartiality in the solution of many urgent local problems. This experience was so successful that a group of business and professional men in Cork proposed having a permanent official, not to replace but to share power with the elected members. The post of city manager was created in Cork CBC in 1929[12] and similar management structures were introduced to Dublin, Limerick and Waterford. Finally, the County Management Act, 1940, brought the management system to the whole country in 1942.

Unlike Britain, where the administrative boundaries of the counties have been altered on more than one occasion, Ireland has had no significant geographic revisions to the organisation of local government since 1898. There is a recognised emotional attachment among the public to the county structure, attributed to the influence of the Gaelic Athletic Association, which organised itself on a county basis from its foundation in 1883[13]. After the publication of the Barrington Report in 1991, consideration was given to the need to retain all eighty smaller urban authorities (borough corporations, urban district councils and town commissioners), the range of whose functions had dwindled over the years. In January 1994, the Minister for the Environment, announcing details of the Government's decision on local government reorganisation at a sub–county level, confirmed the retention of the existing, town–based system because of the strong sense of civic tradition, local identity and loyalty in many urban areas, which the Government perceived as a strength to be built on[14].

In the 1940 Management Act, functions of local government are divided into 'executive' and 'reserved' – the former exercisable only by the manager, the latter by the councillors. The reserved functions are specified in various local government statutes and any power, function or duty not so identified is an executive function[15]. In broad terms, powers reserved to the elected representatives concern policy and political and financial matters, while the manager is responsible for decisions which involve the execution of settled policy and which, in particular, might be open to political or personal influence. Thus, within the planning system, the councillors adopt the development plan and the manager makes the decision whether to grant or refuse individual planning applications.

The introduction of the management system has been the most important single development in the history of Irish local government this century[16]. However, the county councillors did not accept it easily and subsequent legislation, in particular the 1955 City and County Management (Amendment) Act, went some way towards redressing their grievances. Section 4 of this Act gave the elected members the power to direct the manager as to how to perform any of his executive functions. It provides that a local authority may

> by resolution require any particular act, matter or thing specifically mentioned in the resolution and which the local authority or the manager can lawfully

do or effect to be done or effected in performance of the executive functions of the local authority.

Planning and Development Acts 1963–99

The current planning system came into force on 1 October 1964, with the commencement of the Local Government (Planning and Development) Act of 1963. Eight subsequent planning acts[17] were introduced to remedy various deficiencies which became evident in the course of operating the system. A small number of other pieces of legislation have also amended the planning acts, mostly in the course of implementing European directives[18].

All local authorities, except town commissioners, were entrusted with the full range of planning responsibilities in 1964, giving eighty-seven planning authorities for a population of 2.8 million. Under the Local Government (Dublin) Act, 1993, this number increased to eighty-eight with the creation of Fingal, South Dublin and Dun Laoghaire–Rathdown County Councils. In 1996, planning authorities ranged in population from 1,704 (Bundoran Urban District) to 480,996 (Dublin County Borough), while the total population of the country stood at 3.6 million[19]. The manager of a county is also, by virtue of the office, manager of each of the sub–county urban authorities, and thus performs an important co–ordinating role in the context of this multiplicity of small planning authorities. Appendix IV contains a schedule of all planning authorities.

CHAPTER 2

Development Plans

The development plan is the basic policy document of the planning authority in which the planning objectives for the next five years are set out. Each planning authority was obliged to make a development plan within three years of the commencement of the 1963 Planning Act, that is by 1967. Thereafter a development plan must be reviewed, at no greater than five-yearly intervals, and either varied (by alteration, addition or deletion) or replaced by a new development plan. Provision is made for the Minister to extend the period for reviewing the development plan[1], and a plan made outside the statutory deadline without the Minister's prior assent is not valid[2]. A study undertaken by An Foras Forbartha in 1983 indicated that three-quarters of all planning authorities were not keeping to the five-yearly scheduled reviews of their development plans[3]. By 1997, the position had improved substantially, with only 35 per cent of planning authorities having a development plan more than five years old but some of these were seriously out of date, for example Tipperary (NR) and Kildare were still relying on plans adopted in 1990[4]. Making or varying a development plan is a reserved function.

Contents
Development plans are in the form of a written statement supplemented by maps. Plans for cities, boroughs, urban districts and certain towns[5] must contain objectives relating to
(1) zoning of land for residential, commercial, industrial, agricultural or other uses,
(2) traffic, both vehicular and pedestrian,
(3) redevelopment of obsolete areas,

6

(4) preservation and improvement of amenities,

(5) conservation of sites which form part of the European Union's ecological network of protected areas[6],

(6) provision of accommodation for members of the travelling community[7],

(7) protection of structures of architectural interest[8], and

(8) preservation of architectural conservation areas[8].

The objectives which it is mandatory to include in development plans for rural areas are slightly different. In addition to objectives (3), (4), (5), (6), (7) and (8) above, 'rural' or county plans must contain objectives relating to the provision or extension of water supplies and sewerage services.

Both urban and rural planning authorities are given the option of including a wide range of other objectives. The categories here include various roads and traffic matters (for example, new roads and parking), structures (height, floor area, density, building lines, layout, associated parking and so on), community facilities (for example, the provision and siting of schools and churches), and amenities (such as the preservation of buildings and archaeological sites and interior features of buildings). Rural plans may also contain zoning objectives[9].

Procedure

When a development plan has been reviewed, the draft of any variation or new plan is subject to public scrutiny. The draft is placed on exhibition for at least three months, during which time the views of the public must be invited by an advertisement placed in a newspaper circulating in the area. Although not statutorily required, most planning authorities try as well to engage in a process of consultation, by holding public meetings in various towns (in the case of 'rural' authorities) or by having an additional exhibition in some or all of the public libraries, staffed by planners ('urban' authorities). Objections made within the display period are considered by the elected representatives before making the plan, and ratepayers who object have the right to state their case before a person or persons appointed by the planning authority[10].

Various bodies and persons must be individually notified of the making of a draft plan. A copy of the draft must be sent to the prescribed authorities. These include adjoining planning authorities, the relevant regional authority, the Minister for the Environment and Local Government, and various other ministers and organisations whose activities are related to planning (for example the Minister for Arts, Heritage, Gaeltacht and the Islands, An Bord Pleanála and An Taisce). Individual notification must be sent to owners and occupiers of buildings of artistic, historical or architectural interest listed for preservation in the draft, giving details of the structure or internal feature proposed to be preserved. Notice must also be served on the owners and occupiers of land over which it is proposed to preserve a public right of way.

The draft development plan may, but need not necessarily, be altered in the light of public reaction. If a material alteration is made to the draft as a result of such amendment(s), the procedure of exhibition and notification must be repeated with two important limitations. The period for public display and receipt of representations is reduced to one month and objections can only relate to the amendments. Thereafter, the elected representatives may make the development plan either 'with or without the proposed amendment or with such other amendment as...they consider appropriate'[11].

Copies of the adopted plan must be kept available for public inspection and purchase, and a general duty is imposed on each planning authority to take the steps necessary to secure the objectives contained in its development plan.

Role of the Minister

Although the councillors have the function of deciding on the final form of the development plan for their area, the Minister for the Environment and Local Government has what Ronan Keane refers to as a 'general supervisory jurisdiction' in the matter[12]. He may require two or more planning authorities to co–ordinate their development plans in a manner specified by him. He may also require a planning authority to vary its development plan in a specified manner[13]. Neither of these powers has ever been used, but the Minister came under considerable pressure in 1996 from residents of Co. Kildare to use the latter power in respect of decisions taken to zone formerly agricultural land for residential use adjoining the main north Kildare towns. The residents felt that the areas involved – Johnstown (c. 52 acres), Kilcock (c. 200 acres), Clane (c. 120 acres), Maynooth (c. 280 acres) – would unbalance and destroy the character of their towns and asked the Minister to have these decisions reversed. While he did not go this far, Brendan Howlin, TD, the Minister for the Environment at the time, wrote to Kildare County Council indicating that the adoption of any further development plans for towns and villages should be deferred until the Council had prepared a strategy for the future development of the county as a whole. This was the first time a Minister found it necessary to intervene in the process of adoption of a development plan, and it undoubtedly sent a clear signal to other planning authorities that controversial rezoning decisions would not be tolerated by central government which, of course, allocates funding for the infrastructural services necessary to allow development to take place on such lands.

CHAPTER 3

Planning for Amenities

In both urban and rural development plans, it is mandatory to include objectives for the preservation, improvement and extension of amenities. Additional provision is made in Part V of the 1963 Planning Act (as amended) for the protection and development of amenities by means of a variety of orders and other mechanisms.

Special Amenity Area Orders

Planning authorities are empowered, but not obliged, to make a Special Amenity Area Order (SAAO)[1] when an area appears to require an additional level of protection on one of the three following grounds:

- its outstanding natural beauty,

- its special recreational value, or

- a need for nature conservation.

Like the adoption of a development plan, the making of an SAAO is a reserved function. The procedure is more formal, however, reflecting the serious diminution of landowners' rights which results from the making of such an order. Certain developments, otherwise exempted[2] , are removed from this category and made subject to planning permission[3]. Furthermore, no compensation is payable in respect of a refusal of planning permission in an area to which an SAAO relates[4].

Unlike a development plan, an SAAO has to be confirmed by the Minister for the Environment and Local Government after it has been made by the elected representatives. A notice is published in a newspaper circulating in the area, indicating that the order has been made and giving a period of at least one month for objections to be lodged. The order, together with any objections, is submitted to the Minister by the planning authority and, if these objections are not withdrawn, a public local inquiry will be held by an inspector from the Department of the Environment. The Minister must consider the objections and the inspector's report before deciding whether to confirm, modify or refuse to confirm the SAAO. Finally, the confirmed order is laid before the Dáil and Seanad, either of which is empowered to annul the order by resolution. Having made an SAAO, the planning authority must review it at least once in every five year period. This provision both protects the rights of land owners in the area and allows for changing circumstances to be taken into account.

Despite these extensive safeguards, only two SAAOs have been made, while a third is in course of adoption. The first, protecting the Liffey Valley between Chapelizod and Lucan, was confirmed on 8 March 1990, about a week before the opening of the West Link high level toll bridge over the river Liffey[5]. The second, for the North Bull Island and associated amenity lands in Dublin Bay within the functional area of Dublin Corporation, was confirmed on 23 March 1995[6]. On foot of a direction issued by the Minister for the Environment in 1996, Fingal County Council prepared an SAAO for part of the Howth peninsula which has been submitted to the Minister for confirmation. The public inquiry will be held in September 1999.

Conservation Orders
In an area to which an SAAO relates, a planning authority may make a further and more specialised order to preserve from extinction or otherwise protect flora or fauna of special amenity value or interest. Again, this is a reserved function but in this instance, an objector would appeal to An Bord Pleanála. No Conservation Order has ever been made.

Tree Preservation Orders
While objectives may be included in development plans for the protection of woods, trees and shrubs, the principal mechanism available to planning authorities if they wish to secure the preservation of trees for amenity reasons is the Tree Preservation Order (TPO)[7]. Tree felling does not

normally require planning permission. A TPO can prohibit the cutting down, topping, lopping or wilful destruction of individual trees, groups of trees or woodlands, thus giving tree felling the status of development. The TPO can also provide for the granting of consent to felling (subject to conditions) on the same basis as planning permission is granted for all other types of development.

Making a TPO is an executive function and the procedure is relatively simple. Having made a TPO, the planning authority must serve a copy on the owners and the occupiers of the lands and on any person known to be entitled to fell the trees in question. Any of these persons may appeal the making of the order to An Bord Pleanála within a specified period (which cannot be less than one month) and the Board may confirm, modify or annul the order. Thereafter, tree felling may be undertaken with permission, if the TPO so provides. Because the procedure is quite straightforward, TPOs are widely used and 196 were in force at the end of 1997[8].

The rights of third parties are very limited in respect of TPOs. The general public has no right to appeal or make submissions on the making of a TPO and only has a right to appeal felling consents if the TPO makes provision for the exercise of this right[9]. A TPO continues in existence indefinitely and there is no obligation on the planning authority to review it at intervals, although it may be revoked or varied by a subsequent order. It cannot apply to dead, dying or dangerous trees, or to the control of the felling of trees required in compliance with some other statutory obligation. An example of such felling would be where the trees in question have been deemed a hazard under section 70 of the 1993 Roads Act and the road authority has served a notice requiring their trimming or removal.

Some woodlands, both coniferous and broadleaf, were originally planted as a crop on which a financial return would eventually be enjoyed. If a TPO is made to preserve such woodlands, compensation is payable in respect of any blanket refusal to consent to felling. However, if the woodlands in question are declared in the order to be of special amenity value or interest, conditions may be included in a consent, requiring replanting, phased felling and/or the preservation of a specified proportion of the trees, without attracting compensation. In the case of trees not comprised in woodlands, compensation may not be payable in respect of a complete refusal of felling consent, depending on whether the trees are declared to be of special amenity value in the TPO[10].

Other measures protecting amenities

A planning authority may secure the creation of a public right of way either by agreement or compulsorily. Having done so, the planning authority has the responsibility of maintaining the right of way.

Planning authorities can plant trees and shrubs on land not in their ownership, with the consent of the owner, and can assist persons or bodies to carry out amenity planting. Powers are also given to planning authorities to secure the removal or alteration of hedges in the interests of amenity, for example to provide or improve a view.

CHAPTER 4

Development Control

The basic concept underpinning the planning code is that permission must be obtained from the planning authority before commencing development. Development is defined as 'the carrying out of any works on, in or under land or the making of any material change in the use of any structures or other land'[1]. 'Land' in this context includes buildings and land covered with water. Exemptions are given in respect of certain categories of development and these are discussed in Chapter 5.

The application

Part IV of the 1994 Planning Regulations deals with the procedural aspects of obtaining permission from the planning authority.

An application may be made for outline permission, permission or (if outline permission has already been granted) approval. An outline permission is an agreement in principle by the planning authority that development of a specific nature and extent may be carried out but it does not, in itself, authorise the carrying out of any works. Detailed plans must subsequently be submitted to the planning authority and an approval obtained before commencing development. Together, an outline permission and an approval equate to permission. The slower route is generally chosen by applicants who are concerned that their proposal is unlikely to be granted (either as proposed or at all) and, consequently, are reluctant to spend money on having detailed plans prepared until they ascertain the attitude of the planning authority. In this context, pre–application discussions may help to identify the issues involved and possible ways of addressing the potential difficulties. It must be stressed, however, that while pre–application discussions are treated as almost essential by some professionals working in the construction industry, they do not commit the planning authority to making any particular decision.

It is not necessary for the applicant to own the site on which an application is made. Particulars of the applicant's interest must be given as part of the application and, if he is not the owner, the applicant must state the name and address of the owner and have the consent of a person with sufficient legal interest to carry out the proposed development[2].

Under the previous (1977) Planning Regulations, notice of intention to apply for planning permission could be given either in a newspaper circulating in the area or by way of a notice erected on the site. Since May 1994, it has been obligatory to give both forms of notice. The newspaper notice must be published during the two week period before an application is made, while the site notice must be erected on or before the day the application is made and maintained in position for at least one month. The contents of both types of notice are specified in the regulations and include the applicant's name, the nature of the application (that is, outline permission, permission or approval) and the nature and extent of the development. These requirements are intended to ensure that neighbours and the general public know of proposed developments so that they can make representations to the planning authority or, later on, appeal to An Bord Pleanála. Additional requirements designed to facilitate public participation are contained in the regulations. The planning authority must prepare a weekly list giving details of each application received. This list is available in the offices of the planning authority and in all public libraries, including mobile libraries. It is also available to the councillors and, normally for a fee, to any person on request. Furthermore, all planning applications, including third party submissions, can be inspected at the offices of the planning authority during the period in which the application is being assessed and thereafter for a period of five years[3]. From the day the planning authority gives its decision, reports prepared by or for the authority in the course of assessing the application are also available to the public.

The contents of a planning application are set out in the regulations. Certain planning applications must be accompanied by an Environmental Impact Statement (EIS) and almost all applications must be accompanied by a fee.

The decision

The planning authority has a rigid time-frame for giving its decision. It is precluded from making any decision within fourteen days of receipt of a planning application (twenty-eight days if the application is accompanied by an EIS). This provision is designed to ensure that members of the public are not prevented from participating in the planning process by precipitant decision making. On the other hand, if the applicant has not received a decision (be it a permission or a refusal) within two months of submitting a complete and valid application, he is regarded as having received an unconditional permission, which is normally (but not statutorily) referred to as a 'default permission'. This two month period can be extended by a request for additional information, a notice requiring an EIS or the consent of the applicant. Additional information may be asked only once, although clarification can be sought in respect of an unclear submission. There is no mechanism for shortening the fourteen day or twenty–eight day minimum period.

Applications for planning permission are decided by the manager, acting in an executive capacity, and conditions are usually attached to the grant of permission. In dealing with any application, the manager is restricted to considering

- the proper planning and development of the area, including the preservation and improvement of its amenities,
- the provisions of the development plan and of any Special Amenity Area Order,
- an EIS if one is required and any EIS guidelines produced by the Environmental Protection Agency,
- government policy and
- general policy directives made by the Minister.

Under the 1992 Environmental Protection Agency Act, the polluting potential of any development which is subject to an Integrated Pollution Control (IPC) licence may not be taken into consideration by a planning authority.

Although deciding on individual applications is an executive function, the elected representatives are given a statutory role if it is the intention of the planning authority to consider granting permission for a development which would materially contravene the development plan or any SAAO[4]. Prior public notice must be given by the planning authority, any objection must be taken into account by the councillors and a resolution passed by at least three-quarters of the total membership[5]. Revocation or modification of an existing permission is also a reserved function[6] and such a resolution may only be passed if there has been a change in the circumstances relating to the proper planning and development of the area concerned.

The reserved powers of elected members have been used in the past (some would say misused) to require the manager, by resolution under section 4 of the 1955 City and County Management (Amendment) Act, to decide a planning application in a particular way. Usually such resolutions required the manager to grant the permission sought. The 1976 Planning Act tried unsuccessfully to restrain councillors by introducing an element of publicity. Where the manager is of the opinion that the development covered by a notice pursuant to section 4 would amount to a material contravention, the matter must be publicly advertised and objections considered as described above. The attendant adverse publicity in the majority of cases did not generally inhibit councillors, however. The frequency and ease with which section 4 resolutions were passed, the spuriousness of some of the grounds advanced by members proposing such resolutions, and allegations of payments to political parties and to individual councillors had, by the late 1980s, brought the planning process into disrepute. Most section 4 resolutions were viewed with disfavour by all the local residents. Consequently, the practice developed of having controversial section 4 resolutions proposed by councillors from outside the electoral area in question, who might thus expect to escape subsequent retribution at the polls. The 1991 Local Government Act modified section 4 of the 1955 Act, by requiring a 'planning' section 4 resolution to be signed by at least three–quarters of the members for the electoral area where the site is located and passed by three–quarters of the total members of the authority. The former provision makes the proposers of a resolution directly answerable to their disaffected constituents at the next election. These restrictions appear to have curbed the abuse of section 4 resolutions in relation to the planning function.

Planning permission enures for the benefit of the land or structure and passes to any new owner of the land, except where otherwise provided by the permission[7], for example, a condition may restrict occupancy to certain classes of person with a need to live in a rural area. A planning permission normally expires after five years[8], although a longer period may be specified in the permission itself. This time limit refers to the completion, not the commencement, of the development. If work has not commenced, the permission lapses or 'withers', while if work has started but is not finished, it may be possible to extend the duration or 'life' of the permission. Planning authorities are statutorily obliged to grant an extension where the application satisfies certain requirements. In particular, 'substantial' works must have been carried out during the life of the permission. The meaning of 'substantial' is not defined in the legislation but case law has indicated[9] that what constitutes substantial works must be decided in the context of the circumstances and that no rule of thumb (for example 40 per cent to 50 per cent) may be applied. The general public is not given any role in considering applications to extend the duration of planning permissions.

A record of planning applications and decisions is kept by each planning authority and is available for public inspection. Known as the planning register, it incorporates a map and copies of any entry may be obtained for a fee.

An Bord Pleanála

Any person may appeal against a grant or refusal of planning permission. The appellate authority, An Bord Pleanála, is a statutory corporation, established by the 1976 Planning Act to determine appeals, references and certain other matters under the Planning Acts and appeals under the Local Government (Water Pollution) Acts, 1977–90, the Air Pollution Act, 1987 and the Building Control Act, 1990.

An Bord Pleanála consists of a chairman and eight ordinary members, all of whom are full–time, salaried office holders. The chairman is appointed by the Government, for a term of seven years, from three names put forward by a selection committee, composition of which is set out in the 1983 Planning Act. Seven of the eight ordinary members are appointed by the Minister for the Environment from nominations received from various cultural, academic and commercial organisations in the field of planning and development. The eighth is a civil servant from the Department of the Environment. Ordinary members are normally appointed for five years, but their term of office can be shorter at the Minister's discretion. All Board members are precluded by statute from holding any other office or employment in respect of which emoluments are payable.

At the end of 1997, the Board had a staff of seventy–seven. This number included twenty–four inspectors, who carry out site visits, conduct oral hearings and are statutorily required to report with recommendations on all appeals. The Board is not bound by its inspectors' recommendations nor can it delegate its decision–making power to them. Formal decisions on planning appeals are made by at least three members of the Board and, while one of these is authorised to sign the decision, responsibility for its contents rests with the Board members as a whole[10].

Board members and inspectors must make written declarations of their interests in land or in any business, profession or occupation relating to the development of land. A register of such interests is kept at the Board's offices and is available for public inspection. There are statutory prohibitions against the Minister exercising control over any appeal and against any person attempting to communicate with Board members for the purpose of improperly influencing the consideration of any appeal.

Appeals

The 1992 Planning Act was primarily directed at amending the appeals procedure, with the aim of having appeals disposed of more quickly. The general right of appeal contained in the 1963 Planning Act was not restricted in any way. However, the 1992 Act introduced a strict time–frame which must be complied with by every party to an appeal. In addition, an objective was set for the Board: to determine all appeals and matters within a period of four months[11]. Unlike the deadline for local planning decisions, this period can be extended by the Board, acting unilaterally. If it appears to An Bord Pleanála that it would not be possible to determine an appeal within the statutory four months, it can serve notice on the parties giving the extended date and the reasons for the delay. The average time taken to dispose of appeals in the years immediately preceding the introduction of the four month objective decreased from twenty–five weeks in 1990 to twenty–three weeks in 1991 and eighteen weeks in 1992[12].

Whether the appellant is the applicant (first party appeal) or a neighbour, residents' association or other concerned individual or interest group (third party appeal), the full grounds of appeal must be received in the Board's offices within one month of the date on which the planning authority makes its decision[13]. The Board is statutorily precluded from accepting late appeals or any elaboration in respect of an appeal duly received. To be valid, an appeal must also be accompanied by the appropriate fee.

In the case of a third party appeal, a copy of the appeal is given by the Board to the applicant, who has one month to submit comments. Obviously, the planning authority in question is always sent a copy of the appeal and it also has one month to respond. A person who is not a party to the appeal may submit observations to the Board. Any such submission must be received within the period of one month beginning on the date on which the appeal is received by the Board. This option is appropriate in circumstances where a third party was satisfied with the original decision and consequently had no wish to appeal but, on discovering that an appeal has been submitted by the developer, wants to bring his concerns or opinion to the Board's attention. If a specific issue arises in respect of which the Board feels it is appropriate, it has a discretionary power to request a party or observer to make a particular submission on this issue[14]. This entire procedure is carefully balanced to avoid unnecessary delays and consequent financial losses to developers, while affording the opportunities required in natural justice for all parties to present their case and rebut opposing submissions.

Sometimes, parties to an appeal may feel they would have a better chance of explaining their position orally and the legislation has always provided for this. Any party may request an oral hearing of an appeal, on payment of the appropriate fee and on submitting such request within the relevant one month period. The Board has absolute discretion in this regard[15] and will only accede to such a request where the oral hearing would aid its understanding of a particularly complex case or where it considers that significant national or local issues are involved and that written submissions need to be supplemented by an oral hearing[16]. The Board may decide to hold an oral hearing even in the absence of such a request. In the context of the overall volume of appeals, very few oral hearings take place. Two thousand, eight hundred and seventy-three planning appeals were determined by the Board in 1997, a year in which thirty-seven oral hearings took place. However, requests for oral hearings are, in themselves, somewhat unusual. In the same year, requests were received in respect of only 3 per cent of appeals[17].

In considering a planning appeal, An Bord Pleanála is required to have regard to the provisions of the development plan but, unlike the planning authority, may decide to grant permission even if the proposed development materially contravenes the development plan[18]. No further public consultation or even consultation with the elected representatives is required, which can be a cause of local disquiet and of friction with the councillors, even though the Board is required to state the reasons for its decision in all cases. In respect of appeals received since April 1995, the full file (including the formerly confidential inspector's report) is available for public inspection for five years after the decision is given[19]. While this additional element of transparency in the planning system has been welcomed by all parties and by the public, in a case where the inspector has recommended a refusal because of incompatibility with the development plan and the Board grants permission, serious tensions can arise locally. The Board is not required to keep minutes of its meetings[20] or to state its reasons for rejecting any recommendation made by an inspector, which somewhat negates the newly granted transparency.

Judicial review

The decision of An Bord Pleanála, be it a permission or refusal, is final as far as the planning merits of a proposed development are concerned. However, decisions of both planning authorities and the Board are open to judicial review by the High Court. This is sometimes erroneously referred to as an 'appeal' to court when in contemplation by persons dissatisfied with a decision of the Board.

The Supreme Court clearly distinguished judicial review from an appeal in the *Radio Tara* case – 'Judicial review, as the words imply, is not an appeal from a decision but a review of the manner in which the decision was made'[21]. Later on in the same judgement, the Supreme Court set out the respective roles of the Board and planning authority vis-à-vis those of the Courts as follows:

> Under the provisions of the Planning Acts the legislature has unequivocally and firmly placed questions of planning, questions of the balance between development and the environment and the proper convenience and amenities of an area within the jurisdiction of the planning authorities and the Board

which are expected to have special skill, competence and experience in planning questions. The court is not vested with that jurisdiction, nor is it expected to, nor can it, exercise discretion with regard to planning matters.

Judicial review is, therefore, the means by which the legality of an administrative action can be tested before the High Court. It is a two stage procedure[22]. At the preliminary or 'threshold' hearing, an application is made to the Court for leave to apply for judicial review. If leave is granted, the matter proceeds to the substantive hearing, at which the application for judicial review is fully argued and the Court may quash the decision in question by granting an order of *certiorari*.

In addition to amending the planning appeal procedure (as set out above) again with the aim of reducing delays and uncertainties in the planning system, the 1992 Planning Act erected what has been described as a 'formidable hurdle'[23] to the questioning of planning decisions. Since October 1992, any challenge to the validity of a planning permission can only be by means of an application for judicial review, made by motion on notice to all parties to the appeal within two months of the decision[24]. Leave to apply will not be granted by the High Court at the preliminary hearing, unless it is satisfied that there are substantial grounds for contending that the decision should be quashed. The High Court's decision is final and can only be appealed to the Supreme Court on a point of law of exceptional public importance. These statutory provisions are more restrictive than those which apply to judicial review generally and so it is much more difficult to succeed in having a decision on a planning application quashed than it is to challenge successfully any other decision of a local authority.

This, of course, was the intention of the legislature in order to filter out 'speculative or obstructionist litigation'[25] and to ensure certainty for developers while protecting the constitutional rights of those who might, on good grounds, want to question the validity of any planning permission.

CHAPTER 5

Exempted Development

As identified at the beginning of the previous chapter, the central principle of the planning system is that permission is required in respect of the development of land[1]. There are two basic categories of development – carrying out works and making a material change of use. The statutory definition of works is wide, including 'any act or operation of construction, excavation, demolition, extension, alteration, repair or renewal'[2]. Taken literally, it would mean that, for example, a householder replacing roof tiles after a storm, or a factory owner replastering part of a wall after a small accident in the delivery yard, would have to go through the full planning permission procedure before starting to make good the damage done to their property. Obviously, such a requirement would be unwarranted and certain types of minor development by private individuals have been given an exemption from the obligation to obtain planning permission.

The planning code identifies a second and very different category of exempted development on the basis of the identity of the person or body carrying it out[3]. The underlying presumption here is that development by state and local authorities is undertaken in the interests of the common good and, therefore, need not be subject to the same level of public scrutiny as development proposed for private benefit.

Exempted development rights arise from three different parts of the planning legislation.

(1) Section 4(1) of the 1963 Planning Act grants specific exemptions, for example to a planning authority carrying out development within its own functional area and, in certain circumstances, to any person carrying out maintenance works on a building.

(2) Section 4(2) of the 1963 Planning Act enables the Minister for the Environment and Local Government to

make regulations adding classes of exempted development to the list contained in section 4(1) and, in particular, to exempt changes of use within certain broad use classes. The Exempted Development Regulations are contained in Part III of the 1994 Planning Regulations.

(3) Section 2 of the 1993 Planning Act enables the Minister to make regulations excluding particular categories of development by state authorities from planning control. These exemptions are contained in Part XIII of the 1994 Planning Regulations.

State authorities
State authorities are defined as any authority being (a) a Minister of the Government or (b) the Commissioners of Public Works in Ireland[4]. Although no specific exemption was given to these authorities in the 1963 Planning Act, it was assumed by all involved in the operation of the planning system that there was such an exemption. This assumption was based on the statutory requirement that a state authority should consult the relevant planning authority before undertaking the construction or extension of any building[5]. The remit of one state authority, the Commissioners of Public Works, was steadily enlarged during the 1970s and 1980s and among its additional activities was the construction of interpretative or visitor centres in various scenic and sensitive areas, such as the Céide Fields (Co. Mayo), the Boyne Valley (Co. Meath) and Dunquin (Co. Kerry). Although some criticisms were voiced against such visitor centres on grounds of both design and location, most were welcomed by the local communities and the general visiting public.

Two interpretative centres proposed in 1989 and 1991 aroused very strong opposition, however. These were to be in the Wicklow National Park at Luggala and in the Burren National Park at Mullaghmore (Co. Clare). The objectors questioned the assumption that the Commissioners were exempt from the obligation to obtain planning permission. The Supreme Court, in a landmark judgement, held that

the statutory requirement to consult did not relieve the
Commissioners of this obligation[6]. The implications of this
judgement were far-reaching in that no planning
permissions had been obtained for development by any
state authorities since the 1963 Planning Act came into
force on 1 October 1964. Schools, hospitals, army
barracks, prisons and government offices constituted, or
contained elements of, unauthorised development, and all
future government projects would be subject to the full
public scrutiny and objection procedure.

The 1993 Planning Act regularised the position retrospectively, providing that such developments had never
required planning permission. The consultation
requirement in respect of development by state authorities
was repealed, as it was clearly superfluous, and the
Minister was empowered to create exemptions for
development in connection with public safety or order, the
administration of justice, national security and defence.
Part XIII of the 1994 Regulations exempts a wide variety of
state projects from planning control. These range from
those obviously within the statutory parameters, such as
garda stations, prisons, courthouses and premises used for
the operations of the Defence Forces, to the more
questionable projects listed in Class (v) which includes
offices used by the President or the Tánaiste[7]. In keeping
with the general trend towards opening public projects to
greater public scrutiny, the 1994 Regulations make
provision for a procedure of consultation for those
categories of development exempted by reason of their being
carried out by state authorities. Having considered
objections, the authority in question may, however, carry
out its proposal exactly as planned and there is no right of
appeal to an independent body such as An Bord Pleánala.

Local authorities
Local authorities which are planning authorities, that is all
local authorities except town commissioners, have always
enjoyed an exemption for development they carry out in
their own districts. This avoids the absurdity of applying to
themselves for planning permission. A local authority is

prohibited from effecting any development which contravenes materially its development plan[8].

Part X of the 1994 Planning Regulations introduced a procedure of public notice and consultation in respect of a wide range of developments. The classes of development open to public scrutiny since 15 June 1994 include:

• the erection of one or more houses,

• the construction of roads over 100 m in length in urban areas (over 1 km elsewhere),

• the construction of bridges or tunnels,

• the construction of waste water treatment works,

• the use of land as a waste disposal facility.

Just like a private developer, the local authority must advertise its intention to develop in a newspaper circulating in the area but it is not required to erect a site notice. Plans and particulars of the proposed development must be made available for at least one month and submissions can be made within this period and the following two weeks. A report must then be prepared for the elected members, summarising objections and evaluating the proposal. This report must indicate if it is now proposed to proceed with the development in question. When the report is submitted to the councillors, they may, using their powers under the 1955 City and County Management (Amendment) Act, direct that the project is not to be carried out.

Probably the most controversial type of project undertaken by local authorities in recent years has been the development of halting sites for members of the travelling community. Until May 1998, these were excluded from the Part X procedure. Even though a community would be affected by a halting site proposal, and at least some members of that community would have strong feelings about the matter, they had no right to be informed of the proposal or to submit observations on it. Concerns were quite validly expressed that the development of such a controversial type of land use should be subject to the same planning evaluation and the same standards of transparency and public scrutiny as any other local authority project. The development of halting sites was brought under the Part X consultation procedure from May 1998[9].

An obvious difficulty with this system of consultation is that it is not open to an independent appeal. However, the initial proposal is developed by the officials and the objections are considered by the elected members in a procedure which is similar to the adoption of development plans. A right of appeal to An Bord Pleánala could be seen as conflicting with the powers of democratically elected local government.

General exemptions

Under the 1963 Planning Act, complete exemption was given in respect of the use of land for the purposes of agriculture or forestry[10]. Over the intervening years, EU and government policy promoted increased afforestation because of the alternative employment it can provide in rural areas, as well as the contribution it can make as a renewable resource. However, by the late 1980s it had been recognised that afforestation can give rise to environmental problems such as visual intrusion, acidification of water and feelings of human isolation. In February 1990, afforestation projects over 200 ha in area were made subject to both planning permission and Environmental Impact Assessment (EIA)[11] and this threshold was reduced to 70 ha in October 1996[12]. It was anticipated that the majority of afforestation projects would still remain outside statutory controls because of their size and, from May 1996, a procedure of consultation between planning authorities and the Forest Service of the Department of Agriculture, Food and Forestry (which is now part of the Department of the Marine and Natural Resources) was instituted in respect of all afforestation projects over 25ha for which grant applications were received. The effectiveness of these arrangements is being monitored and is due for review in 1999[13]. Use of previously uncultivated land for intensive agricultural purposes, where an area of more than 100 ha is involved, and peat extraction involving new or extended areas greater than 50ha, have also been subject to EIA and planning controls since 1990.

The other exemption given in the 1963 Planning Act of general significance is for

> Development consisting of the carrying out of works for the maintenance, improvement or other alteration of any structure, being works which affect only the interior of the structure or which do not materially affect the external appearance of the structure so as to render such appearance inconsistent with the character of the structure or of neighbouring structures.[14]

Whether the external appearance is affected for better or worse is not at issue here. The central question relates to the character of the structure and to whether the works are inconsistent with that character. The Supreme Court has indicated that the character of a terraced house is much more dominantly affected by its street appearance than its rear appearance and that the elements which go to make up the character of a structure are its shape, colour, design, ornamental features and layout[15]. Relying on this definition, it was held that replacing Georgian style, timber, 'up and down' sash windows with aluminium, 'swing opening' windows was inconsistent with the character of Victorian houses on Belgrave Square in Dublin[16]. This decision was of importance in terms of conservation, because window replacement is a type of 'improvement' which can be carried out very quickly with disastrous consequences for the visual amenities of an area[17].

The majority of exempted developments carried out by private individuals are those described in the Second Schedule to the 1994 Planning Regulations, that is, small structural works over which detailed control is considered unnecessary. Examples of the type of domestic exemptions which are provided for in the Planning Regulations are building a small extension (including a conservatory) or a front porch, converting a garage, erecting a greenhouse or garden shed and hard surfacing part of a garden as a patio (to the rear) or a parking area (to the front). Exemptions are also given for the erection of boundary walls on both domestic and other property, for different types of advertisements and for agricultural buildings. Exactly what falls within or outside the terms of the various exemptions is much clearer here. Detailed descriptions are given of each class of exempted building, together with the applicable conditions and limitations, and the works themselves are visible and measurable.

However, the Schedules must be read together with Part III of the Regulations, in particular Articles 9 and 10, because notwithstanding the fact that a particular development might fall exactly within the scheduled description, it loses its exempted status if any of the restrictions set out in Article 10 apply. Thus, for example, permission must be obtained if the development would contravene a condition of a planning permission, involve a new access to a public road, create a traffic hazard, break the established building line (except for a front porch) or involve works to a building listed for preservation in the development plan.

An amount of controversy has arisen in relation to one particular type of exemption. The 1994 Planning Regulations granted a six month exemption from May 1994 for the carrying out of various types of telecommunications developments[18]. In the 1994–96 period, the rapid growth of the mobile telecommunications service gave rise to significant planning pressures, as a multiplicity of applications was received for the antennae required for transmitting telephony signals and their support structures, base stations and ancillary services. Draft Planning Guidelines were issued by the Department of the Environment for discussion in December 1995 and finalised in July 1996[19]. These emphasised the importance of co-location by operators to avoid the unnecessary proliferation of masts. In February 1997, amending regulations[20] gave statutory support to this policy by creating two new classes of exempted development:

(1) attachment to an existing radio mast of antennae for mobile telephony, and

(2) replacement of existing masts.

Both are subject to a number of conditions and limitations. In particular, the number of such antennae may not exceed twelve and additional antennae cannot be larger than those already on the mast, while replacement masts shall not exceed the height of the original.

Development enjoying the benefit of these new exemptions has consisted largely of the replacement by licensed operators of outdated support structures at garda stations. The operators can then avail of the exemption to attach their antennae for private mobile telephony onto the new mast. Local communities have expressed serious concerns at the possibility of health risks as a result of radiation emissions emanating from such multiplicity of antennae. They also suspect that some masts are being replaced by taller structures. An interlocutory injunction to stop the erection of a mast and base station at the garda station in Easkey, Co. Sligo, was sought unsuccessfully in 1998 by a group of children attending the adjoining national school[21], while other communities have resorted to protest action at the sites of such development.

As set out at the beginning of this chapter, a material (that is substantial) change of use also constitutes development. The 1994 Regulations create exemptions for certain changes of use. A number of use classes are set out in the Second Schedule, and development which consists of a change of use within any one of these classes does not require permission. Again, the exempted status is withdrawn if the development would contravene a condition of a planning permission, be inconsistent with a use specified in a permission or involve carrying out works other than those which are themselves exempted development.

Accordingly, under Class 2, it is possible to change from a bank to a building society, insurance broker's or solicitor's office without obtaining a grant of permission, because all these are activities principally offering services to visiting members of the public. A change of use from a shop to such a direct service would require permission. Use as a shop is a Class 1 activity and the impact in planning terms of a shop is considerably different from that of a financial services office. The façade of a shop taken over, for example, by a building society will be changed from a display of goods for sale to a series of notices setting out interest rates. These businesses have the ability to pay high rents for high profile locations with good pedestrian flows but have a sterilising effect on shopping streets. Therefore, any such change of use must be subject to specific assessment in the light of the development plan and requires planning permission[22].

References

The concept of exempted development involves mixed issues of law and fact. If a question arises as to what, in any particular case, constitutes exempted development, the 1963 Planning Act provides that the matter shall be referred to and decided by An Bord Pleanála. Unlike the position with a planning permission, where only the manner in which the Board reached its decision is open to judicial scrutiny, there is a right of appeal to the High Court against the Board's determination of an exempted development reference[23]. The planning authority has no statutory role in deciding questions relating to exempted development although the staff of many planning offices are prepared to offer guidance if queries are raised with them. Advice given in these circumstances is merely an opinion and cannot bind the planning authority to any subsequent course of action[24].

The number of references dealt with annually by An Bord Pleanála is very small by comparison with the number of planning applications. Fifty references were received by the Board in 1996 and this number was reduced to forty–two in 1997[25].

CHAPTER 6

Enforcement

The requirement to obtain planning permission before commencing development is supported by a range of statutory sanctions. In addition to imposing the obligation to obtain planning permission, the 1963 Planning Act provided that any person carrying out unauthorised development would be guilty of an offence[1]. As prosecution and conviction do not secure the proper planning and development of the area but merely the punishment of wrongdoers, planning authorities were also given power to implement planning controls by means of enforcement notices which require developers to conform to the planning code.

Initially, control of unauthorised development was solely a matter for planning authorities, which were not required to take action in all cases but were given the power to serve an enforcement notice 'if they decide it is expedient to do so'[2]. Proceedings on foot of such a notice are a District Court matter. District judges were reluctant to convict landowners who pleaded that they had been unaware of the new requirement to obtain permission, explained that on receiving the enforcement notice they had applied for permission to retain the development as constructed and were confident of obtaining such a permission. A series of adjournments might be granted if the proposal was appealed and, as set out in Chapter 4, the appeal time–frame was open–ended until the 1992 Planning Act brought in the four month objective. The delays and the small fines which could be imposed by the Court meant the enforcement notice procedure was ineffective in controlling unauthorised development of a serious nature.

The Planning injunction
The 1976 Planning Act created a new and important form of

enforcement action, which has come to be known as a section 27 or planning injunction[3]. The most significant aspect of this type of action is that it is available not only to the planning authority but also to any member of the public, irrespective of having an interest in land or being able to claim to be suffering particular damage from the development in question. Injunctions of their nature are obtainable quickly. The jurisdiction was vested in the High Court, which took a much stricter approach towards breaches of the planning code than the District Court had done. Failure to obey an injunction constitutes contempt, an offence punishable by imprisonment. These four features of the planning injunction meant that it was an extremely significant addition to the mechanisms for planning control.

The procedure had one unfortunate limitation. If a planning permission had been obtained but was not being complied with in carrying out development (either through disregarding conditions or for any other reason), the Court could make whatever order was necessary to ensure conformity with the permission, including ordering that building work done be demolished. However, a person who completely disregarded the legislation and did not get any planning permission was in a stronger position. In these circumstances, the High Court had prohibitory powers only and, while it could grant an injunction restraining the continuance of the illegality, it could not order the developer to undo the works he had carried out.

From the perspective of planning authorities attempting to enforce the planning code and aggrieved neighbours distressed by what they perceive to be the destruction of their environmental amenities, this was a particularly frustrating anomaly. The 1992 Planning Act remedied the position, providing that whether or not permission has been obtained, the Court can grant both mandatory and prohibitory injunctions and, in so far as is practicable, order that land be restored to its condition prior to the commencement of the unauthorised works or change of use. A planning injunction can now be applied for in the Circuit Court as well as in the High Court, which opens the remedy to a section of the general public who might have been hesitant to approach the High Court because of the costs involved. The 1992 Planning Act also introduced a five year time limit on applications for this statutory injunction, bringing the procedure into line with other types of enforcement action.

Warning notice
The 1976 Planning Act further strengthened the powers of planning authorities against unauthorised development by introducing a procedure which enabled them to take action at a much earlier stage than had been possible with enforcement notices. A warning notice may be served on a landowner, where it appears that unauthorised development is being or is likely to be undertaken, including removal of or damage to a tree or feature required to be preserved as a condition of a planning permission[4]. The notice brings the breach or apprehended breach of the planning code to the landowner's attention and sets out exactly what must be done to comply with the legislation (discontinuance, non-commencement or protection as appropriate). It warns the landowner to take adequate steps to ensure compliance and that proceedings may be brought against him if he fails to do so. Copies of the notice may be given by the planning authority to any other person concerned with the matter, such as an employee or sub-contractor.

Failure to comply 'knowingly' with the requirements of a warning notice constitutes an offence, as does 'knowingly' assisting or permitting the carrying out of the relevant development. The penalties are extremely severe. A person convicted on indictment under this section is liable to a fine of up to £1 million or to imprisonment for a term not exceeding two years, or to both. Continuation of the offence after conviction constitutes a further offence and further penalties apply.

Enforcement notices
Since the Planning Act came into operation on 1 October

1964, it has been open to planning authorities to take action against developments

(1) for which no permission has been granted or for which permission has been granted, where any condition has not been complied with[5],

(2) for which permission has been granted, where the development has not been or is not being carried out in conformity with the permission[6],

(3) for which retention permission has been granted, where any condition has not been complied with[7].

A notice may be served on the owner and the occupier of the land, specifying the breach of planning control and detailing the steps which are necessary to regularise the position. A period of at least one month must be allowed for compliance, after which (if the required steps have not been taken) the planning authority is empowered to take action against the developer. The penalties are not particularly severe, being punishable by a maximum fine of £1,000, with a maximum fine of £200 per day for a continuing offence[8].

The enforcement notice procedure is the option most frequently availed of by planning authorities to control unauthorised development. The Department of the Environment's *Planning Statistics 1997* indicates that 874 cases were initiated under (1) above and compliance with the notice was secured in 541 of these. Eighty–five notices were served under (2) above and compliance was secured in all cases[9]. (The figures in respect of (3) are too small to warrant comment).

CHAPTER 7

Compensation

The principle of planning compensation is that, if the value of an interest in land is reduced as a result of a planning decision, the person having such an interest is entitled to be paid, by way of compensation, an amount representing this reduction in value. The reduction could arise either from a refusal or from a permission with onerous conditions. Generous provisions were made in the 1963 Planning Act with regard to both eligibility for compensation and amounts awarded.

There are no provisions about betterment in the present planning code. The provisions in the 1934 Act never came into operation and experience elsewhere was not encouraging. The Act of 1963 does, however, provide for contributions to planning authorities from developers for benefits derived from public services[1].

It must be borne in mind that, while compensation is payable by the planning authority, the decision on which it is grounded will almost always have been one taken by An Bord Pleanála on appeal.

The Constitutional issue

The 1963 Planning Act had to be drafted in the light of the rights to private property contained in Bunreacht na hÉireann (Constitution of Ireland, 1937). Article 43 guarantees to pass no law attempting to abolish the right of private ownership, while recognising that the state may delimit the exercise of private property rights by law in the interests of the common good.

Compensation was provided for in Part VI of the 1963 Planning Act. With very limited exceptions (principally refusals on traffic safety, sanitary or other public health grounds), if the value of an interest of a landowner was reduced as a result of a refusal of permission or a grant subject to conditions, the landowner was entitled to be paid compensation. Ronan Keane, now a judge of the Supreme Court, expressed the opinion that without these provisions for the payment of compensation 'the constitutionality of the far-reaching interference with property rights which the Acts permit would be in question'[2].

That the legislature was correct to be concerned about the constitutionality of the 1963 Planning Act was quickly evident. In March 1968, less than four years after the act had come into force, proceedings were issued by a number of property owners in Dublin city centre, claiming that the powers given to planning authorities in relation to development plans were unconstitutional. This challenge was unsuccessful, largely because the High Court found that the legislation provided compensation for the refusal of permission to construct buildings on undeveloped land, except in very limited circumstances based on the 'exigencies of the common good'[3].

A compensation culture
The operation of the planning system developed very much in the shadow of this and another High Court judgement. In the *Viscount Securities* case, it was held that a refusal for permission to build houses on land zoned for the further development of agriculture created a liability for compensation[4]. After this second decision in 1976, there was a gradual awareness among development industry advisers that any purchase of land could lead to a valid compensation claim, even if it failed to lead to a permission for housing. There was a similar awareness among planners that every refusal was being made in the shadow of possible claims, which could be avoided only by the inclusion of non-compensatable reasons. This set a very low value indeed on the provisions of democratically adopted development plans.

In the mid 1980s, a more environmentally conscious public began to become aware of the magnitude of compensation claims. The much publicised payment by Dublin County Council of £1.871 million compensation to a property company, Grange Developments, after a vigorously challenged claim, aroused considerable opposition to what was perceived as unjust enrichment of private developers out of public funds. Planners and lawyers began asserting the opinion that a change to the Planning Acts, eliminating payment of compensation in respect of developments contravening the zoning provisions of development plans, could be justified in constitutional terms. The argument was made that a development plan, which provides for the control and encouragement of development in a manner benefiting the community, represents the embodiment of the 'common good' and that limiting the right to develop in contravention of such a plan was justified without compensating the landowner for loss of the development value of the land in question. This represented a fundamental shift in attitude from the pre–eminent position given earlier to every aspect of the rights of land ownership.

Interpretation of the Constitution by the judiciary reflects the changing standards of society and judicial indication was given by the Supreme Court in December 1986 that reconsideration of the constitutional constraints on the planning system was possible. In the *X.J.S. Investments* case, 24 acres of land at Roches Hill in Killiney, which had been bought in 1981 for £40,000, were the subject of a compensation claim in the order of £2.375 million arising out of a refusal of permission for a residential development on the lands. The land was zoned for open space in the development plan and the proposal contravened this zoning objective. In his judgement, Judge McCarthy specifically drew attention to the question 'as to whether or not legislation which appears to authorise such a use of public funds is constitutionally proper'[5].

Restrictions
The 1990 Planning Act came into force on 10 June 1990 and completely changed the position regarding compensation. The balance, hitherto in favour of the individual landowner, was now tilted in favour of the planning authority, as can be seen from an examination of the Department of the Environment's most recent edition of *Planning Statistics*. In 1990, claims for compensation to the

value of £41 million were lodged, while just five small claims amounting to £2.3 million were registered in 1997 and all were disposed of. Fingal County Council is the only area which continues to be affected by any significant level of compensation claims. It received three claims totalling slightly over £2 million in 1997 and had three claims amounting to £3.7 million outstanding at the end of that year[6].

The non-compensatable reasons for refusal were enlarged significantly. In particular, if permission is refused for development on the grounds that it would contravene materially the zoning provisions of the development plan, this refusal no longer attracts compensation. If zoning is changed, landowners have five years to bring forward development proposals of a type which would have been acceptable under the former zoning. During this period, it would be open to a landowner to claim compensation in respect of a refusal of such an application on zoning grounds. This provision is intended to afford reasonable protection to landowners who have seen the value of their land reduced as a result of 'down-zoning'. An examination of the full list of non-compensatable reasons for refusal indicates the increased importance of the development plan as a basis for the restriction of property rights.

The 1990 Planning Act also introduced new valuation rules for the assessment of planning compensation. It should be pointed out that compensation paid under the planning code does not transfer ownership of the land in question to the planning authority. Prior to 1990, the same valuation rules applied to compulsory purchase, purchase notices, open space acquisition[7] and planning.

The size of awards pre 1990 resulted from compensating landowners for 'potential' loss – the loss of value which could have been realised if the permission had been granted. The new valuation rules are specifically designed to assess the reduction in value resulting from a planning decision. This reduction is the difference between the antecedent and the subsequent values of the land[8], where these are the open market values before and after the decision. Planning compensation continues to be assessed by the property arbitrators appointed under the Property Values (Arbitrations and Appeals) Act, 1960.

Another very significant route by which a landowner might become eligible for compensaion was through the sanitary services legislation. Permission could be refused for development which was premature because of existing deficiencies in water supply or sewerage facilities, without liability for compensation arising. However, the Supreme Court held, in the *Shortt* case, that a landowner had a statutory right under the 1878 Public Health (Ireland) Act to connect to a public sewer, provided that there was adequate capacity in the sewer to accept the foul water in question[9]. It was immaterial that the sewer had been designed to service the planned and orderly development of designated lands. A refusal on the grounds that the available capacity was reserved for future development on other lands attracted compensation.

The 1990 Planning Act removed the absolute right of connection, making it dependent on the consent of the sanitary authority[10]. A grant of permission is taken to include such consent and in considering whether to grant consent/permission, consideration can be given to the requirements of other parts of the authority's functional area and to other prospective developments.

Notice preventing compensation

If a claim for compensation is received by a planning authority, the authority may within three months serve a notice on the claimant, stating that the land in question is capable of other development for which permission ought, in the opinion of the planning authority, to be granted[11]. The effect of such a notice is to prevent the payment of compensation on foot of the claim. The notice continues in force for a period of five years, unless within this period it is withdrawn by the planning authority or annulled by reason of the specified development being refused.

CHAPTER 8

Acquisition

The Planning Acts do not, in themselves, contain any specific powers of compulsory acquisition[1], but planning authorities are given wide powers to develop or secure the development of land[2]. For example, they can enter into joint ventures with private developers and, generally, act as development corporations/property managers in their own functional areas, providing sites for the establishment and relocation of industries and businesses (including hotels, offices and shops), factory and other commercial buildings and any ancillary services considered necessary. A review of the operation of the planning system carried out in 1983 found planning authorities to have been most successful in the acquisition and development of land for the establishment or relocation of industry[3]. Their lack of enthusiasm for using their full range of development powers has been commented on as recently as 1998, planning authorities being referred to as still 'somewhat reluctant developers in their own right'[4].

The planning code provides two procedures whereby land can be acquired by a planning authority.

Purchase notice
Section 29 of the 1963 Planning Act is intended to give some redress to a person whose land is incapable of 'reasonably beneficial use' in its existing state and who will not be granted permission to develop in a manner which would give him a reasonable income from the property. In what can be seen as the reverse of compulsory purchase (where the local authority designates the land to be acquired), a landowner who, on appeal, has been refused permission or received a conditional grant of permission, may serve a notice on the local authority, requiring it to purchase his interest in the land, if he can claim

(a) that the land has become incapable of reasonably beneficial use in its existing state,

(b) that the land cannot be rendered capable of reasonably beneficial use by carrying out any other development for which permission has been granted, and

(c) if the purchase notice is based on a conditional grant of permission, that the land cannot be rendered capable of reasonably beneficial use by carrying out development in accordance with that permission.

The notice must be served on the planning authority within six months of the grounding decision. The planning authority may decide to comply with the purchase notice, in which case it indicates its acceptance to the landowner within three months. This notice of acceptance has the same effect as a confirmed Compulsory Purchase Order and the planning authority must acquire the interest in question.

If the planning authority is unwilling to comply with the purchase notice, within three months it must indicate its reasons to the landowner and send these together with the purchase notice to An Bord Pleanála. The Board has a wide range of powers and can confirm or refuse to confirm the notice, grant permission for the refused development, revoke or amend the conditions objected to or direct that a 'beneficial' permission be granted for all or part of the lands. Only a small number of purchase notices fall to be determined by the Board annually – five in 1997 and four in 1996[5]. A planning authority must acquire the landowner's interest if the purchase notice is confirmed by An Bord Pleanála.

'Reasonably beneficial use' is not defined in the legislation and the meaning of the term is not at all clear. There is very limited Irish case law in this area but some guidance can be obtained from English decisions. It has been suggested that the relevant criteria include the physical state of the land, its shape, size and surroundings and the general pattern of land use in the vicinity[6].

Acquisition notice

Section 25 of the 1976 Planning Act, like section 27 which introduced the planning injunction, strengthened the armoury of the planning authority in dealing with unauthorised development.

A problem which arose quite frequently in relation to residential developments in the late 1960s and early 1970s was that the developer would build and sell the houses while, at best, ignoring the area designated for public open space and, at worst, treating it as the site dump. The developer would then abandon the site with serious consequences for the amenities of the area.

Since November 1976, where permission has been granted for a development and the provision of open space was either required by conditions or implicit or explicit in the application, the satisfactory completion of the development can be secured by the planning authority. A notice may be served on the landowner, detailing the works necessary to make the relevant area suitable for the purpose for which it was intended. A period of at least two months must be allowed for compliance, after which the planning authority may commence the compulsory acquisition of the land designated as open space. The procedure is relatively straightforward and far simpler and quicker than compulsory purchase.

A notice is published in a newspaper circulating in the district (the acquisition notice) indicating that it is the intention of the planning authority to acquire the land and specifying that an appeal may be made to An Bord Pleanála. An appeal period of at least two months must be allowed. Any person with an interest in the land may appeal, and the Board can annul the acquisition notice or confirm it, with or without modification. If there is no appeal or the Board confirms the notice, the planning authority may proceed to acquire the land by means of a Vesting Order procedure[7]. Only under exceptional circumstances will a landowner recover compensation for an acquisition under this section[8].

CHAPTER 9

Regional Planning

Neither regionalisation nor regional planning were mentioned in the 1963 Planning Act but the intention to construct a regional framework was part of ministerial thinking while the Bill was still on its way through the Dáil and Seanad. During the Seanad debate the Minister said:

> It is my aim that, following on the passage of this Bill, regional studies should be made with strong support and guidance from my Department in order that the economic objectives of planning that I have outlined will be pressed forward vigorously. Other countries in Europe are using physical planning to advance their economic development and we cannot afford to ignore their example. Indeed, I regard this as probably the most important long–term task facing the local authorities in this country...[1].

Regional development organisations

When the Bill became law the Minister grouped the counties into nine physical planning regions, to facilitate the co-ordination of development plans, and appointed consultants to prepare advisory reports on two of them – the Dublin Region (Professor Myles Wright of Liverpool) and the Limerick Region (Nathaniel Lichfield and Associates). Subsequently, in an attempt to resolve the sensitive issue of selectivity with regard to centres of growth, Colin Buchanan and Partners, in association with An Foras Forbartha, were asked to complete regional studies for the rest of the country[2].

The Buchanan Report was published in 1969 and regional development organisations (RDOs) were established in each of the nine planning regions the same year. These unelected bodies consisted of representatives of local authorities (both councillors and managers), various other state–sponsored organisations and the Minister for Local Government. The function of the RDOs was 'to co–ordinate the programmes for development in each region'[3] and their first task, the production of regional development reports, was concluded in the early 1970s. Despite little commitment to them from either local or central government, which of course was reflected in limited allocation of resources, the RDOs continued in existence until 1987, mainly to co–ordinate the work of the various state development agencies.

Regional authorities

Regional planning was finally put on a statutory basis by the 1991 Local Government Act which empowered the Minister for the Environment to establish regional authorities 'for the purpose of promoting the co–ordination in different areas of the State of the provision of public services'[4]. In January 1994, eight such authorities were established covering the entire country. Membership is composed of city and county councillors selected by the constituent authorities and, in his press release on their establishment, the Minister for the Environment carefully reassured the local authorities that these regional bodies would not diminish or restrict their powers. The regional authorities have been given two functions: (i) promoting the co–ordination of the provision of public services on a regional basis, and (ii) monitoring/advising on the implementation at regional level of the various Operational Programmes for delivery of European Union Structural and Cohesion Funds. A schedule of the regional authorities is contained in Appendix V.

As part of its co–ordinating role, a regional authority is required

- to review, from time to time, the development plans of local authorities in its functional area, and

- within two years of being established and thereafter at five-yearly intervals, to prepare a regional report covering the overall development needs of the region, the review of development plans and the provision of public services[5].

By mid 1996, all eight regional authorities had produced a report. The approach taken to the mandatory review of constituent development plans varied greatly in these reports and it has been noted that where planners had a strong input into the report's preparation, the final document reflected a corresponding strength in terms of spatial issues[6]. In particular, the South West Regional Authority included a detailed summary of each of the constituent development plans and its proposals were strongly reflective of these plans. The Midland and the Dublin Regional Authorities also reviewed a wide range of issues relating to development plans. The Dublin Regional Authority highlighted a number of inconsistencies among local authority development objectives and set out issues of regional significance[7].

The regional authorities are not statutorily empowered to take strategic decisions. Although a number of them 'interpreted their mandate liberally'[8], enlarging their brief to produce reports which, in some cases, are explicitly plans and, in others, have a considerable degree of policy content[9], the regional reports are of persuasive value only.

In 1999, a non–statutory report of far more planning significance on the regional scale was drawn up for the local authorities in the greater Dublin area, in conjunction with the Dublin and Mid–East Regional Authorities. The *Strategic Planning Guidelines for the Greater Dublin Area* were prepared at the initiative of the Department of the Environment, to provide an overall strategic context for the development plans of the relevant planning authorities and to provide a framework for investment in sanitary services, transportation and other infrastructure[10]. The guidelines set out a logical development strategy of maintaining a compact metropolitan area while developing strong growth centres in the hinterland. Many of the policies contained in the guidelines will be delivered through the development plans of the constituent local authorities. Launching the guidelines, the Minister for the Environment and Local Government said that he was committed to their implementation and that he intended 'to formally request each local authority to ensure that their development plans are fully in line with the strategy'[11].

Such a request could of course be issued under the 1963 Planning Act[12] and would be binding on the authorities concerned. No request or direction has been issued to date but it has been agreed that the structures set up for the preparation of the Strategic Planning Guidelines will, in broad terms, remain in place for the necessary monitoring and review process. The two regional authorities have given the guidelines unanimous approval, and support for them has been expressed by some of the constituent local authorities.

Regional Assemblies
Regional planning was given a new impetus in mid 1998, with the discovery that recently achieved national prosperity would exclude Ireland from the highly desirable Objective 1 status under the next round of EU structural funding (2000 – 06). In November 1998, after an extended period of political consultations, the Government proposed to divide the country into two regions to ensure that the poorer counties, which still had incomes below the EU threshold for Objective 1 areas, could continue to draw down the maximum level of European funding. It was initially thought that this would result in some genuine devolution of power, if only to satisfy the requirements of the European Regional Affairs Commissioner[13].

Fifteen counties were selected for inclusion in the 'disadvantaged' or 'west coast' region. These were the counties forming the functional areas of the existing Western, Midland and Border Regional Authorities plus counties Kerry (South West) and Clare (Mid West). The Government was able to show clear differences in relative wealth between the west and east of the country, with dependency on agriculture much higher in the west which had not experienced a level of economic growth similar to that of the east over the period of the 1994–99 National Development Plan. After assessment by Eurostat, the independent statistical service of the European Commission, the Minister for Finance announced to the Dáil in March 1999 that, subject to modifications (the elimination of counties Kerry and Clare), the proposal to regionalise the country had been accepted by the Commission. In April 1999, development strategies for each of these approved regions were published as inputs to the 2000–2006 National Plan[14] on behalf of a joint committee representing the existing regional authorities in each of the NUTS II regions[15].

To give effect to the new regionalisation, two assemblies were established as and from 21 July 1999, with membership drawn from the existing eight regional authorities[16]. The Border, Midland and Western Regional Assembly, which is to have its headquarters at Ballaghadereen, Co. Roscommon, will have twenty-nine members, while the Southern and Eastern Regional Assembly, located in Waterford City, is to have forty-one members. The functions of the new assemblies centre mainly on the promotion of co-ordination among local, regional and other public authorities. However, the Minister for Finance may request these assemblies to manage Operational Programmes under the National Development Plan 2000–06 and to monitor and make proposals in relation to matters of EU financial assistance[17].

Members are to be nominated, therefore linkage with the general public will be tenuous. Because the existing regional authorities remain unchanged, there will now be four layers of administration (central, supra–regional, regional and local) and it remains to be seen if the assemblies will have any impact on planning in their functional areas. As constituted, the only relevant planning responsibility they have been given is the somewhat peripheral role of considering 'from time to time, the reviews of the development plans of local authorities in the region as carried out by the relevant regional authorities'[18].

CHAPTER 10

Urban Renewal

By the mid 1980s, urban dereliction had reached crisis level and the country was in recession. In 1985, Dublin was described as 'probably the shabbiest, most derelict city in Europe' with 'evidence of urban blight everywhere – 'weed–strewn sites surrounded by decaying hoardings, dilapidated buildings boarded up and left to face the elements and gap–toothed streets'[1]. Other cities and towns were suffering comparable levels of urban decay. Development plans had made various attempts to secure the renewal of obsolete areas but had had little impact on the property market. The success of the tax incentives package, introduced jointly by the 1986 Urban Renewal Act and the 1986 Finance Act, in bringing about private sector investment demonstrated the inherent linkages between fiscal policy and physical redevelopment. Obsolete areas, which had stubbornly failed to regenerate despite special policies in development plans permitting higher densities and commercially more favourable mixes of land uses[2], became desirable sites and were renewed within a short period of the introduction of the financial incentives.

The three models
Under the two 1986 Acts and the 1991 Temple Bar Area Renewal and Development Act, three models for urban renewal were established. The most radical, particularly in terms of the interface of fiscal-led urban renewal and planning, was that applied in the Custom House Docks Areas of Dublin.

An area of some 27 acres on the north side of the River Liffey, defined in the Schedule to the 1986 Urban Renewal Act, was granted an exemption from the planning control exercised by Dublin Corporation in respect of development consistent with a planning scheme approved by the

Minister for the Environment. A separate development authority, the Custom House Docks Development Authority (CHDDA), was established in November 1986[3] to promote and secure the redevelopment of this area. Given powers to acquire, hold and manage land, including by compulsory purchase, this non–elected body enjoyed in effect the status of a separate planning authority until its dissolution in May 1997[4]. The 1987 Urban Renewal (Amendment) Act enabled the Custom House Docks Area to be extended by Ministerial Order. The first such order in July 1987 extended the Custom House Docks Area to the centre of the River Liffey and two further orders increased its area to 74 acres (including water) between then and May 1997. The area covered by these two orders is currently undergoing redevelopment[5].

The CHDDA was solely an urban renewal agency concerned with the physical regeneration of its area and was successful in meeting its objectives on these terms. However, the planning scheme procedure, under which a master plan for the redevelopment of the Custom House Docks Area was to be prepared, allowed for public participation on a far more limited basis than would be the case with a local authority type development plan. Once a scheme was approved by the Minister, development which was certified by CHDDA as being consistent with it did not have to go through the planning application process, but constituted exempted development[6]. The Custom House Docks Area had thus been removed from the control of the democratically elected local authority. This model of urban renewal, while extremely efficient, was remote from the wider community in terms of organisational structure and resulted in a form of development with weak physical links to the rest of the city[7]. It was also criticised for underlining existing disparities between different socio–economic groups in our society[8].

In the Budget statement of January 1996, the Minister for Finance announced the Government's decision to adopt a strategic approach to the renewal of the adjoining and now mainly redundant Dublin docklands, which cover a large area on both sides of the river Liffey. A task force was immediately established to report on the arrangements necessary to develop a master plan for the docklands and on appropriate implementation and co–ordination mechanisms[9]. It concluded that a new form of organisation was required for the docklands area to provide an appropriate level of democratic and community involvement in the master plan process. The government accepted these recommendations and directed the CHDDA to set up a project team to take forward the preparatory works for a master plan while the necessary legislation was being prepared. Three preparatory studies on the land use, architectural heritage and socio–economic structure of the area were completed later the same year as a basis for the master plan[10]. Another report entitled 'Towards a Master Plan', was commissioned to expedite the process and, by the time the Dublin Docklands Development Authority (DDDA) was established in May 1997, the master plan was at an advanced stage of preparation.

The functions of this authority are to secure:

- the social and economic regeneration of the docklands area on a sustainable basis,

- the improvements of the physical environment of the docklands area, and

- the continued development in the CHDDA of the financial services sector[11].

Members of the DDDA are unelected, as was the case with the CHDDA, but in addition to ministerial appointees the membership includes five city councillors. The master plan was drafted in partnership with local residents and community groups, business and sectoral interests, environmental and cultural organisations, Dublin Corporation, other statutory bodies and training agencies. After a one month display period, the master plan was adopted, with a number of amendments and modifications, in November 1997. This master plan was in turn taken into consideration by the Corporation in the preparation of the 1999 Dublin City Development Plan[12]. A number of minor differences in relation to parking standards and zoning were addressed and resolved in the course of adopting the city plan. Both the planning authority and An Bord Pleanála are required to consider the provisions of the master plan when assessing any planning applications in the docklands area[13]. Thus, the democratic deficit in the CHDDA model has been overcome while ensuring that a comprehensive, integrated approach is adopted to the promotion and control of development in this large and significant urban renewal area.

With the enactment of the 1997 Dublin Docklands Development Authority Act, the Custom House Docks Area was subsumed into the much larger Dublin Docklands Area, which covers approximately 526 ha (1300 acres) north and south of the River Liffey. While planning exemptions continue to apply for those areas formerly exempted under the approved 1987 and 1994 Planning Schemes for the Custom House Docks, most of the lands covered by these schemes had been developed by 1997. Like its predecessor, the DDDA also enjoys in effect the status of a planning authority as far as the Custom House Docks Area is concerned and it is empowered to use a planning scheme procedure largely similar to that which was mandatory in the Custom House Docks Area, either within that area or for any other part of the docklands if the Minister by order specifies the lands in question as suitable for the planning scheme procedure[14].

Significantly, if such a procedure is to be used for any part of the docklands other than the original Custom House Docks Area or those lands lying between Guild Street and East Wall Road south of Sheriff Street (which could be seen to form a geographic extension of the Custom House Docks area), the relevant order must be laid in draft form before the Oireachtas and both Houses must pass a resolution approving the order[15]. Therefore, it is highly unlikely that the development of any of the docklands, outside this 'enlarged' Custom House Docks Area, will be removed from the normal planning process.

In September 1998, the Minister extended the Custom House Docks Area to include approximately 30 acres between Guild Street and New Wapping Street, consisting principally of lands formerly used as railway marshalling

included in the lands designated along both sides of the
Quays under the 1986 legislation. This area was extended
by the 1991 Temple Bar Area Renewal and Development
Act[18], which also established two companies with
complementary roles in the area's rejuvenation.

Temple Bar Properties, a development company with
the Taoiseach as its sole shareholder, was created to
acquire, hold, manage and dispose of land for
redevelopment, either by itself or by others. In particular,
it acquired some nine acres of CIE's property and
commissioned the preparation of a Framework Plan for the
area which, although not statutory, provided the basis for
the redevelopment programme. Unlike the CHDDA, Temple
Bar Properties was not given any special planning powers
and Dublin Corporation, as planning authority, continued
to be responsible for the control of development in Temple
Bar.   Temple Bar Renewal was established to approve
existing or proposed buildings for tax incentives and, under
the 1991 Act, was precluded from approving certain uses
considered unsuitable for the type of urban regeneration
needed to establish a Cultural Quarter, for example,
incentives were not available for warehouses or for factories
over a certain size. Temple Bar Renewal will be wound up
when the tax incentives for the area end and its residual
functions have been completed. At present, the deadline for
availing of tax incentives has been extended to December
1999. However, because of the number of cultural centres
developed using European funding and the number of
activities in occupation under licence, Temple Bar
Properties may continue with a town centre management
role for a period after it has achieved the objective of
securing the redevelopment of its property in the area. No
decisions have yet been taken on the final management
structure for the Temple Bar Area but it is possible
responsibility will be transferred to the local authority,
which could establish some form of semi–autonomous body
for this purpose.

In the CHDDA, the tax allowance in respect of capital
expenditure on construction/refurbishment of commercial
buildings was 100 per cent, as in provincial cities, whereas

in the remainder of the designated areas in Dublin it was 50 per cent. The other incentives consisted of a double rent allowance against trading income for businesses leasing new or refurbished commercial buildings, and remission of rates, both of these reliefs being available for ten years. Owner–occupiers received an allowance against income tax in respect of 50 per cent of expenditure on the construction/refurbishment of dwellings, also over a ten year period. Investors received 100 per cent relief against tax on rental income, in respect of construction/refurbishment of residential property for letting, provided they retained the property for ten years. The specific range of tax incentives introduced in the 1991 Finance Act for Temple Bar were more generous than those available elsewhere and were particularly designed to secure investment in refurbishment.

Urban renewal evaluated

In 1996, the Department of the Environment commissioned the carrying out of a study on the impact and effectiveness of the urban renewal schemes[19]. Recognising that urban renewal in Ireland had become 'inextricably linked to tax incentives'[20], the consultants concluded that, in the future, measures and programmes for urban renewal must also be linked to area–based, integrated, strategic planning. One of the difficulties identified in the study was that the existing statutory development plans were prepared on too large a scale to address the type of planning necessary for targeted urban renewal to be achieved. The Temple Bar Framework Plan was cited as the type of small scale, localised plan needed to avoid piecemeal redevelopment and to facilitate and guide urban renewal. Another issue identified was the process of selection of areas for designation. Criteria had not been set out in the 1986 legislation and the boundaries of designated areas had been drawn up by the Department of the Environment (or, in the case of Temple Bar, by the Department of the Taoiseach) in consultation with the relevant local authorities, by a simple process of broadly defining areas in need of rejuvenation. The consultants recommended that, in the future, designation should not

between 500 and 6,000 and, like the 1999 Urban Renewal Scheme, will adopt a focused approach, in this case based on Town Renewal Plans. Guidelines for the preparation of these plans, which are based on the IAP formula but adapted to take account of differences of scale and socio–economic function, have been circulated to all county councils. The Town Renewal Plans are to be completed by 1 November 1999 and, again, will be assessed by the expert advisory group. Designated status may be granted to individual buildings, groups of buildings or sub–areas within the context of those plans approved by the Minister on the basis of the advice of the expert advisory group. There will be a strong emphasis on refurbishment and residential investors will receive tax incentives only where absolutely necessary to achieve the objectives of the plan. The implementation of the scheme will have to wait for the necessary provisions to be included in the Finance Act for the year 2000 and it is envisaged that the scheme will run initially for three years from early in 2000.

The Town Renewal Scheme reinforces recent legislation on the protection of architectural heritage described in Chapter 11[23]. A highly unsustainable form of development in recent years, which has given rise to one of the most intractable planning issues throughout the country, has been the sprawl along rural roads of bungalows occupied by families who work and attend school in nearby towns. The Town Renewal Scheme is aimed at countering demand for one–off housing in the countryside by making small settlements attractive places to live (as they once were) rather than the mere daytime services centres they have become since the 1960s[24]. It will also assist in increasing the housing supply in accordance with principles of sustainability because tax incentives will be targeted where infrastructure is already available.

Following the recommendations of the KPMG–led study in 1996, both the 1998/9 Urban Renewal Scheme and the 1999 Town Renewal Scheme follow the Temple Bar model in two aspects. The IAPs and Town Renewal Plans, which translate development plan policies into area action plans, target particular problems and identify designations needed in consultation with local partnerships and communities. The scale and highly focussed approach of these plans draws on the successful experience of the Temple Bar Framework Plan. Qualification for tax incentives is subject to certification by the relevant local authority that the development complies with the objectives of the IAP or Town Renewal Plan. This puts local authorities in a position analogous to that of Temple Bar Renewal Ltd. The integrated area/town renewal plan approach to designation for tax incentives is giving both urban and rural local authorities a leading role in the promotion and implementation of urban regeneration within their own functional areas.

Seaside resorts

By 1994, the first and second generation urban renewal schemes[25] had achieved considerable success in securing the physical redevelopment of the main cities and provincial towns. Since the 1970s, changing patterns in the holiday market, competition from cheap European 'sun' destinations together with rising standards of demand for accommodation and facilities, had all combined to push the traditional, small seaside resort towns into a downward spiral of decline. Seeing the success of tax incentives in larger urban areas, Bord Failte and the Department of Tourism and Trade concluded that a comparable scheme was essential to secure the regeneration of seaside towns. From an extensive list supplied by Bord Failte, fifteen seaside resorts were designated in the 1995 Finance Act, following consultations between the Department of Tourism and Trade (the sponsoring department in this case), Regional Tourism Managers, Shannon Development, the Department of the Environment, the Department of Finance and a number of local authorities. As with the initial urban renewal schemes, criteria for establishing the extent of designation were not contained in the legislation. Instead, the exact boundaries of the designated resort areas were decided at the same time as the resorts were identified and using the same consultation mechanism. These boundaries were then set out in the 1995 Finance Act along with the list of resorts.

authorities of any expertise or capability to deal with marine issues needs to be addressed.

A significant area at the interface of the planning system and marine resource management is the licensing of aquacultural activities. Because these activities are located on the foreshore, the planning authority has no direct control over them and yet such developments can have an adverse impact on the functional area of the planning authority in terms of visual intrusion, pollution, etc[4]. Ancillary land–based facilities, such as processing units and storage buildings, are of course, subject to normal development control. Applications for aquaculture licences (finfish and shellfish) are made to the Minister for the Marine and Natural Resources and a person aggrieved by the Minister's decision can appeal against it to the Aquaculture Licences Appeals Board[5]. Among the factors which both of these licensing authorities must take into account are the provisions of the relevant development plan[6]. When an application for an aquaculture licence is received, the Minister must inform the local authority contiguous to whose functional area the proposed aquaculture is to take place[7]. Planning authorities thus have two formal opportunities to influence the site selection process of aquacultural activities.

Building control

Under the 1878 Public Health (Ireland) Act, sanitary authorities were empowered to make bye–laws controlling the construction of buildings (building bye–laws). This legislation was availed of by only a handful of authorities, such as the main cities of Dublin and Cork[8]. Under the 1963 Planning Act, the Minister for Local Government (as he then was) could make building regulations but, while various drafts were published for consultation, no such regulations were made and it was not until 1992 that a system of building control became operational throughout the country.

The 1990 Building Control Act is principally enabling legislation. It gives the Minister power to make regulations relating to public policy issues such as access for disabled people and conservation of fuel and energy[9], in addition to regulations directed at controlling the quality of building works. The first nationally applicable building regulations, the 1991 Building Regulations, came into force in June 1992[10]. They were amended and consolidated, with effect from July 1998, by the 1997 Building Regulations[11].

The Building Regulations are divided into twelve sections setting out technical requirements for the design, construction and alteration of buildings under a variety of headings such as structure, fire safety and access for disabled people. These requirements are written as broad functional statements and are backed up by a series of twelve Technical Guidance Documents, the purpose of which is to provide advice on compliance with the regulations. The primary responsibility for compliance rests with the parties involved – designers, owners and builders – and the requirements of any of the provisions of the regulations can be met by alternative means. However, where works are carried out in accordance with the guidance contained in the Technical Documents this will, *prima facie*, indicate compliance.

The Building Control Regulations prescribe the procedures to be followed in order to comply with the Building Control Act. These regulations have also been amended and consolidated. The 1997 Building Control Regulations[12] came into force in July 1998. Not all local authorities are building control authorities under the 1990 Act. In principle, the function was given only to the larger local authorities (the county council and county borough corporations) as well as to any local authority which was already a fire authority[13]. Building control authorities do not certify any aspect of works, except fire safety and then only for buildings other than dwelling–houses, but they have powers to inspect building works and plans. They also have powers of enforcement and prosecution.

As with the planning code, certain classes of development are exempted from control but the exemptions under the two systems are not the same.

- the revised definition of a derelict site[20], which includes dwellings and was intended to overcome problems caused by the more restrictive definition in the earlier legislation,

- the requirement that all local authorities establish a derelict sites register by June 1991 and thereafter maintain same,

- the power given to local authorities to serve notices on landowners specifying measures to be taken to avoid dereliction, which works constitute exempted development under the planning code,

- improved powers of acquisition and

- the introduction of a derelict sites levy.

Environmental impact assessment

Environmental impact assessment (EIA) is the term applied to the systematic examination of the likely impacts of development proposals on the environment prior to the initiation of any development works. It does not pre–determine whether or not development takes place but ensures that where effects are identified which would be unacceptable, these can then be avoided or reduced[21].

The European Directive on the Assessment of the Effects of Certain Public and Private Projects on the Environment[22] was implemented in Ireland by the 1989 European Communities (Environmental Impact Assessment) Regulations[23]. Being necessitated by the state's obligation to comply with community law, as a member state of the EU, these regulations could amend an existing statute[24]. Accordingly, the 1989 Environmental Impact Assessment Regulations, which came into operation in February, 1990, grafted environmental impact assessment in respect of private projects onto the planning application procedure. An amending Directive in 1997[25] was transposed into Irish law by the 1999 European Communities (Environmental Impact Assessment) (Amendment) Regulations, as and from 1 May 1999. There are now five sets of Regulations on environmental impact assessment which must be construed together and the Department of the Environment hopes to have them consolidated later this year.

Two terms are used frequently in relation to EIA – 'screening' and 'scoping'. Screening means determining when a project requires EIA, while scoping focuses attention on the appropriate aspects of the project in question[26].

Planning applications for developments specified in the First Schedule to the EIA Regulations must be accompanied by an environmental impact statement (EIS)[27]. Some of the projects listed in Part II of the First Schedule are defined by means of a threshold. For example, Class 10 includes industrial estate development projects where the area exceeds 15 ha. Screening, therefore, is carried out principally by the listing of project types and the definition of thresholds in the First Schedule.

However, planning authorities are empowered to require the applicant to submit an EIS for a scheduled project, notwithstanding that it is under the defined threshold, if they consider that the development would be likely to have significant effects on the environment[28]. Planning authorities may also require an EIS in respect of any type of development proposed for an environmentally sensitive site[29]. Neither of these provisions constitutes a requirement for case–by–case examination of all relevant projects. Selection criteria are set out in the Third Schedule to the EIA Regulations and these constitute the basis for screening, in relation to both environmentally sensitive sites and sub–threshold projects.

An EIS must contain the information specified in the Second Schedule to the EIA Regulations. These include a description of the development proposed, the data required to identify and assess the main effects which that development is likely to have on the environment, an outline of the main alternatives studied by the developer and a description of the aspects of the environment likely to be affected (biological, geophysical and social). A summary of this information in non–technical language must also be submitted[30]. This last element is very important because

EISs are, of their nature, highly complex documents and
third parties could be effectively excluded from the planning
process if its adaptation to incorporate EIA made core
information virtually indecipherable in respect of the largest
and most significant development proposals.

Even prior to the introduction of the 1999 EIA
Regulations, in sub–threshold cases pre–application
discussions almost always took place with the planning
authority staff, to identify if an EIS would be required and,
generally, to determine the scope of the requisite EIS.
Experience has shown that EIA is facilitated by effective and
early scoping, in which the issues of actual concern are
identified and given the appropriate emphasis[31]. Since 1
May 1999, this process has been put on a formal basis[32]. A
prospective applicant is entitled to obtain a written opinion
on the information to be contained in an EIS from the
planning authority within a set time-frame, which should
not exceed ten weeks. It remains to be seen if the
hard–pressed planning authorities, who are dealing with
ever–increasing numbers of planning applications, can keep
to this schedule.

The procedural aspects of EIA as it relates to planning
applications are covered in Part IV of the 1994 Planning
Regulations, as amended. If a planning application is
accompanied by an EIS, this must be stated in the
newspaper notice and an outline application cannot be
made in respect of a project which is subject to EIA. Copies
of any EIS submitted as part of the planning application
process, and of extracts therefrom, must be available for
purchase at the offices of the planning authority.

The Environmental Protection Agency
The Environmental Protection Agency (EPA) was
established in 1993 under the 1992 Environmental
Protection Agency Act to carry out a wide range of functions
relating to the environment, such as monitoring
environmental quality, providing support and advisory
services to local authorities and promoting environmental
research[33]. The most important planning related
function of the Agency is the licensing, regulation and

control of a wide range of industrial–type activities. The implementation of this type of licensing from May 1994 represented an important new advance in environmental protection.

Under earlier legislation (such as the Water Pollution Acts 1977–90 and the Air Pollution Act, 1987), discharges were licensed by local authorities and each environmental medium had its separate standards. Reducing the impact on one medium under one legislative code could have adverse consequences elsewhere. The main objective of integrated pollution control (IPC) licensing is to prevent or solve pollution problems rather than transfer them from one part of the environment to another. A single licence is issued to cover all aspects of air, water, waste and noise, in recognition of the fact that the environment functions as an integrated whole[34]. The range of activities subject to IPC licensing has been expanding steadily since 1994.

If a proposed development constitutes an activity subject to IPC, neither the planning authority nor An Bord Pleanála can take the risk of environmental pollution into account in assessing the proposal[35]. The polluting potential of such an activity is uniquely within the competence of the EPA. It was anticipated by those involved in the operation of the planning process that this separation of powers would present difficulties but the experience has been largely positive to date[36].

Nature conservation
Two European Directives have been specifically aimed at nature conservation, the Directive on the Conservation of Wild Birds (the 'Birds Directive') and the Directive on the Conservation of Natural Habitats and of Wild Flora and Fauna (the 'Habitats Directive')[37]. The latter is one of the most ambitious pieces of European legislation. It provides for the establishment of a network of protected sites across all Member States. Sites are to be selected in accordance with scientific criteria specified in the Directive.

Incorporation of the Habitats Directive into Irish domestic law has been highly problematic because of the impact it will inevitably have on marginal agricultural holdings. The Directive was implemented in February 1997 by the European Communities (Natural Habitats) Regulations[38], and the process of designating sites, known as Special Areas of Conservation, has been in operation since then.   One hundred and thirty–eight sites have completed the national designation process and have been notified to the European Commission by the Department of Arts, Heritage, Gaeltacht and the Islands[39], which has responsibility for the implementation of these two Directives. There are two further stages in the designation process. The Commission, in agreement with the Minister, will select sites from this list for adoption as sites of Community importance and, finally, the Minister will designate such sites as Special Areas of Conservation[40].

Over one hundred Special Protection Areas under the Birds Directive have been designated during the period since 1985. Together, Special Areas of Conservation and Special Protection Areas are referred to as European Sites. In relation to the planning process, once sites have been adopted as being of Community importance (the second stage), it is mandatory to include objectives in development plans for their protection.   In the course of assessing relevant planning applications, consideration must be given to the impact of the development proposed on such adopted sites, normally but not exclusively by means of an EIS.

CHAPTER 12

The Flood Tribunal

In October 1997, the Oireachtas passed a resolution establishing a tribunal under the Tribunals of Inquiry (Evidence) Act 1921 (as amended), to investigate certain planning matters following the making of allegations that payments of money had been made to politicians and/or officials in the functional area of the former Dublin County Council[1], in order to procure favourable planning decisions[2]. Claims that corrupt land rezoning was taking place had been made persistently over a number of years and a reward of £10,000 had been offered anonymously through a Newry–based firm of solicitors in 1995 for information leading to convictions.

The terms of reference of the tribunal limited its inquiry geographically to 726 acres of land at six separate locations in Finglas (two sites), Poppintree, Donabate, Balgriffin and Portmarnock, and were based on a letter written in 1989 by Michael Bailey to James Gogarty concerning these lands and how to procure planning permission for their development. The second and related issue identified for inquiry was the matter of payments to political parties, members of the Oireachtas, members or officials of the Dublin local authorities or any other public official by the said Messrs Gogarty and Bailey. In relation to either matter, the tribunal was only empowered to investigate events which occurred on or after 20 June 1985. The Minister for the Environment and Local Government appointed Mr. Justice Feargus M. Flood, who had been a High Court Judge since 1991, as the Chairman and sole member of the tribunal in November 1997. Mr. Justice Flood began his work in December of the same year, assisted by a team of lawyers and administrators.

The terms of reference of the tribunal were amended in July 1998 in two respects.

(i) The limitation on reporting acts of which the tribunal became aware in the course of its inquiries but which took place before 20 June 1985 was removed, although this date remained as the commencement date for investigations. Thus, events which in the tribunal's opinion amount to corruption or involve attempts to compromise the disinterested performance of public duties, no matter when they occurred, are to be included in the tribunal's final report to the Clerk of the Dáil.

(ii) Specific inquiry was to be made into payments to a former Minister, Raphael Burke, from any source and unfettered by any time-frame.

Apart from preliminary sessions in 1998 to hear applications for legal representation by various interested parties, the tribunal carried out its investigations in private until January 1999 when public hearings began in Dublin Castle. To date, thirty–six witnesses have given evidence. It may be anticipated that the work of the tribunal will continue until at least the end of the year 2000.

Chapter 1

1. Keane, Ronan (1982), *The Law of Local Government in the Republic of Ireland*, Dublin: Incorporated Law Society of Ireland, p.149.

2. Nowlan, Kevin, I. (1989), 'The Evolution of Irish Planning, 1934–1964' in M. J. Bannon (ed), *Planning – the Irish Experience 1920–1988*, Dublin: Wolfhound Press, p. 71.

3. Ibid., p.80. The three counties which did not feel it necessary to give themselves planning powers under the 1934–39 Acts were Longford, Mayo and Offaly.

4. Section 29 of the 1934 Town and Regional Planning Acts reflects the leisurely pace of development in that decade. It reads as follows 'when a planning authority has decided under this Act to make a planning scheme, such authority shall with all convenient speed give effect to such decision and make a planning scheme in accordance therewith and shall submit such scheme to the Minister for approval'.

5. Purcell, Matthew (1964), *Guide to the Local Government (Planning and Development) Act, 1963*, Dublin: Incorporated Law Society of Ireland, p. 4.

6. *The State (Modern Homes) v Dublin Corporation* (1953) IR 202.

7. Purcell, *op. cit.*, p. 5.

8. Nowlan, *op. cit.*, p. 85.

9. 1963 Planning Act, Second Schedule.

10. Tipperary was already divided into two 'ridings' under the Grand Jury system. Consequently, two councils were established here in 1898, one in the North Riding and one in the South Riding. Yet, Co. Tipperary has a single 'identity' which can be traced to the influence of the GAA (see p. 3 *infra*).

11. Chubb, Basil (1992), *The Government and Politics of Ireland*, London: Longman, p. 269.

12. Cork City Management Act, 1929.

13. Tierney, Myles (1982), *The Parish Pump*, Dublin: Able Press, p. 18.

14. Department of the Environment Press Statement, 27 January 1994.

15. County Management Act, 1940, s. 17.

16. Keane, *op. cit.*, p. 18.

17. For a full list of the Planning Acts and a summary of the principal amendments contained in each, see Appendix I.

18. The Environmental Impact Assessment Regulations are listed in Appendix III. The impact of these and of other environmental and related legislation is discussed in Chapter 11.

19. Census of Ireland, 1996.

Chapter 2

1. 1963 Planning Act, s. 20(1A) inserted by s. 43 of the 1976 Act.
2. While s. 20(1A) of the 1963 Planning Act, inserted by s. 43(1)(f) of the 1976 Planning Act, empowers the Minister to extend the five year period within which a development plan must be reviewed, there is no mechanism whereby the Minister can retrospectively extend this period in order to validate a plan adopted after its expiration. There is no restriction on either (i) the length of extension the Minister can grant or (ii) the number of times the Minister can extend the plan–making period.
3. Grist, Berna (1984), *The Preparation of Development Plans*, Dublin: An Foras Forbartha, pp. 3–6.
4. Department of the Environment (1998), *Planning Statistics 1997*, pp. 45–46.
5. These are the towns listed in the First Schedule to the 1963 Planning Act. The basis on which they were selected is largely irrelevant in 1999, with some urban settlements which were only villages in 1963 having outgrown neighbouring scheduled towns.
6. Objective added by 1997 European Communities (Natural Habitats) Regulations, Article 26(b).
7. Objective added by 1998 Housing (Traveller Accommodation) Act, s.26.
8. Both these objectives were added by the 1999 Planning Act, s. 33. This Act does not come into operation until January, 2000. For a discussion on the changes brought about by the 1990 Planning Act, see Chapter 11, *Built Heritage, infra* p.66.
9. The word 'zoning' is not used in the Planning Acts although it has been generally adopted to convey the more cumbersome legal phrase 'use solely or primarily (as may be indicated in the development plan) of particular areas for particular purposes (whether residential, commercial, industrial, agricultural or otherwise)' which is contained in the 1963 Planning Act, s. 19.
10. The rated occupier of a dwelling who no longer actually pays rates, because of the relief granted by the 1978 Local Government (Financial Provisions) Act, remains a ratepayer for the purposes of this provision of the planning code.
11. 1963 Planning Act, s. 21(A), inserted by s. 37 of the 1976 Act. The 'other' amendment presumably would be a compromise position of some form.

12. Keane, *op. cit.*, p. 154.
13. 1963 Planning Act, s. 22(2).

Chapter 3

1. 1963 Planning Act, ss. 42–43 as amended by s. 40(a) of the 1976 Act.
2. For a discussion of exempted development under the planning code, see Chapter 5, *infra*, p.24.
3. 1994 Planning Regulations, Article 10(1)(b).
4. 1990 Planning Act, s. 12(1) and Second Schedule, paragraph 6.
5. Dublin County Council (Lucan Bridge to Palmerstown) Special Amenity Area Order (Confirmation) Order, 1990 (SI 59 of 1990).
6. North Bull Island Special Amenity Area Order, 1994 (Confirmation) Order, 1995 (SI 70 of 1995).
7. 1963 Planning Act, s. 45, as amended by s. 40(b) of the 1976 Planning Act and s. 21 of the 1990 Planning Act.
8. Department of the Environment (1998) *Planning Statistics 1997*, Table 39.
9. *Wicklow County Council v An Bord Pleanála*, (1990) 8 ILTR. 107.
10. 1990 Planning Act, s. 21, as amended by s. 21 of the 1992 Planning Act.

Chapter 4

1. 1963 Planning Act, s. 3.
2. In the case of *Frescati Estates v Walker* (1975) IR 177, the Supreme Court held that an application for permission must be made either by or with the approval of a person who has 'sufficient legal estate or interest to enable him to carry out the proposed development'. See also Article 18 of the 1994 Planning Regulations.
3. 1994 Planning Regulations, Article 36.
4. 1976 Planning Act, s. 39(d).
5. 1991 Local Government Act, s. 45.
6. 1963 Planning Act, s. 30.
7. 1963 Planning Act, s. 28(5).
8. 1982 Planning Act, s. 2.
9. *Frenchurch Properties Ltd. v Wexford County Council* (1992) 2 IR 268.
10. See the Chairman's Statement on page 2 of An Bord Pleanála's *Annual Report 1996*, for a brief description of their decision making process.

11. 1992 Planning Act, s. 2.
12. An Bord Pleanála: *Report and Accounts 1992*, p. 18.
13. 1992 Planning Act, s. 3.
14. 1992 Planning Act, s. 9.
15. 1992 Planning Act, s. 12.
16. An Bord Pleanála: *Annual Report 1997*, p. 11.
17. *Ibid.*, p. 11 and p. 17.
18. 1976 Planning Act, s. 14(8).
19. 1995 (No. 2) Planning Regulations, Article 2 (SI 75 of 1995).
20. *O'Keefe v An Bord Pleanála* (1993), 1 IR 39.
21. *Ibid.*, at p. 71.
22. Rules of the Superior Courts, Order 84 (SI 15 of 1986).
23. Macken, James (1997), 'Judicial Review of Planning Decisions', *The Bar Review*, vol. 2, issue 4, Dublin: Bar Council, p. 127.
24. 1992 Planning Act, s. 19(3).
25. Macken, *op. cit.*, pp.127-8.

Chapter 5

1. 1963 Planning Act, s. 24.
2. 1963 Planning Act, s. 2(1).
3. Galligan, Eamon (1997), *Irish Planning Law and Procedure*, Dublin: Round Hall Sweet & Maxwell, p. 84.
4. The definition of State authorities given in section 84 of the 1963 Planning Act included the Irish Land Commission. The 1993 Planning Act repealed s. 84 and contains the amended definition.
5. 1963 Planning Act, s. 84(1).
6. *Howard v the Commissioners of Public Works* in Ireland (1994) 1 IR 101.
7. 1994 Planning Regulations, Article 156(1)(a).
8. 1963 Planning Act, s. 39.
9. 1998 Planning Regulations (SI 124 of 1998).
10. 1963 Planning Act, s. 4(1)(a).
11. The 1989 Environmental Impact Assessment Regulations (SI 349 of 1989) gave the Minister power to prescribe development which would thus be removed from the category of exempted development. The Minister exercised this power in Article 11 of the 1990 Planning Regulations (SI 25 of 1990). The named types of development also became subject to Environmental Impact Assessment as they were specified in the First

Schedule, Part II of the EIA Regulations. Article 13 of the 1994 Planning Regulations repeated Article 11 unchanged.

12. 1996 Planning Regulations, Article 3 (SI 100 of 1996) and 1996 Environmental Impact Assessment Regulations, Article 3, (SI 101 of 1996).

13. Department of the Environment (1997), *Forestry Development – Consultation Draft Guidelines for Planning Authorities*, p. 11.

14. 1963 Planning Act, s. 4(1)(g).

15. *Cairnduff v O'Connell* (1986), ILRM 465.

16. *Dublin Corporation v Bentham* (1993) 2 IR 58.

17. For a discussion of the possibility of controlling window replacement, see Grist, Berna (1998), 'Building Conservation Under the Planning Code', *Irish Planning and Environmental Law Journal*, vol. 5, no. 4, Dublin: Round Hall Sweet & Maxwell, p. 140.

18. 1994 Planning Regulations, Article 9(1)(b) and Second Schedule, Part I, Class 29.

19. Department of the Environment (1996), *Telecommunications Antennae and Support Structures – Guidelines for Planning Authorities*, Dublin: Stationery Office.

20. 1997 Planning Regulations (SI 78 of 1997).

21. *Szabo v ESAT Digiphone Ltd* (1998), 2 ILRM 102.

22. For a general analysis see Grist, Berna (1994), 'Exempted Development under the 1994 Planning Regulations', *Irish Planning and Environmental Law Journal*, vol. 1, no. 2, Dublin: Brehon Publishing Ltd., p. 51.

23. 1963 Planning Act, s. 5.

24. *Dublin Corporation v McGrath*, unreported, High Court, 17 November 1978, McMahon, J.

25. An Bord Pleanála: *Annual Reports 1996*, p. 21 and 1997, p. 20.

Chapter 6

1. 1963 Planning Act, s. 24(3).

2. 1963 Planning Act, s. 31(1)(a).

3. 1976 Planning Act, s. 27, as substituted by s. 19(4)(g) of the 1976 Act.

4. 1976 Planning Act, s. 26.

5. 1963 Planning Act, s. 31.

6. 1963 Planning Act, s. 35.

7. 1963 Planning Act, s. 32.

8. 1992 Planning Act, s. 20.

9. Department of the Environment (1998), *Planning Statistics 1997*, Tables 24 and 24A, pp. 23–24.

Chapter 7
1. Roche, Desmond (1982), *Local Government in Ireland*, Dublin: Institute of Public Administration, p. 203.
2. Keane, R., op. cit., p. 195.
3. *Central Dublin Development Association v Attorney General*, 109 ILTR 69.
4. *Viscount Securities Ltd. v Dublin County Council*, 112 ILTR 17.
5. *X.J.S Investments Ltd. v Dun Laoghaire Corporation* (1987), ILRM 659.
6. Department of the Environment (1998), *Planning Statistics 1997*, p. 36.
7. Purchase notices and acquisition notices are discussed in Chapter 8, *infra*.
8. 1990 Planning Act, First Schedule, Rule 1.
9. *Dublin County Council v Shortt* (1983) ILRM 377.
10. 1990 Planning Act, s. 25.
11. 1990 Planning Act, s. 13.

Chapter 8
1. For a clear explanation of the legal position in this regard, see Keane, op. cit., pp. 223–4. See also Nowlan, Kevin (1978), *A Guide to the Planning Acts*, Dublin: Incorporated Law Society of Ireland, p. 102.
2. 1963 Planning Act, s. 77.
3. Grist, Berna (1983), *Twenty Years of Planning*, Dublin: An Foras Forbartha, p. 11.
4. O'Sullivan, P. and Shepherd, K. (1998, 8th issue), *Irish Planning Law and Practice* edited by M. O'Donnell, Dublin: Butterworths, para 1.102.
5. An Bord Pleanála, *Annual Reports, 1997*, p. 20 and *1996*, p. 21.
6. Galligan, E., op. cit., p. 338.
7. See Keane, op. cit., p. 206 and also p. 261.
8. McDermott, S. and Woulfe, R. (1992), *Compulsory Purchase and Compensation in Ireland: Law and Practice*, Dublin: Butterworth (Ireland) Ltd., p. 311.

Chapter 9
1. Roche, op. cit., p. 200.

2. For an analysis of this period in Irish regional planning, see Bannon, Michael J. (1989), 'Development Planning and the Neglect of the Critical Regional Dimension' in M. J. Bannon (ed), *op. cit.*, pp. 122–157.

3. Government Statement, 19 May 1969.

4. 1991 Local Government Act, s. 43.

5. Local Government Act, 1991 (Regional Authorities) (Establishment) Order, 1993, Article 14 (SI 394 of 1993).

6. van der Kamp, Hendrik and Bannon, Michael J. (1997), 'An Overview of the Regional Reports' in D. McCafferty and J. A. Walsh (eds.), *Competitiveness, Innovation and Regional Development in Ireland*, Dublin: Regional Studies Association (Irish Branch), p. 287.

7. Dublin Regional Authority (1996), *Dublin: A Regional Focus*, p. 61.

8. van der Kamp, H., and Bannon, M.J., (1997), *op. cit.*, p. 287.

9. *Ibid.*, p.288.

10. *Strategic Planning Guidelines for the Greater Dublin Area* (1999), prepared by Brady Shipman Martin and Others for the Department of the Environment and the Local and Regional Authorities in the Greater Dublin Area.

11. Department of the Environment Press Statement, 25 March 1999.

12. See Chapter 2, *Role of the Minister, supra*, p.8.

13. During a visit to Dublin in September, 1998, Commissioner Monika Wulf–Mathies gave an interview to Radio Telefís Éireann in which she outlined her opposition to Member States making cosmetic changes to their internal structures in order to increase funding allocations. In a memorable soundbite, the Commissioner described this type of approach as 'subsidy shopping'. (*The Irish Times*, 18 September 1998).

14. Fitzpatrick Associates Economic Consultants, (April 1999), *Border , Midland and Western Region Development Strategy 2000–2006* and (April 1999) *Southern and Eastern Region Development Strategy 2000–2006.*

15. The Nomenclature of Territorial Units for Statistics (NUTS) was established by Eurostat to provide a single, uniform breakdown of territorial units for the production of regional statistics for the European Union.

16. Local Government (Regional Authorities) (Establishment) Order, 1999, Article 5 (SI 226 of 1999).

17. *Ibid.*, Article 15(1)

18. *Ibid.*, Article 14(2)(d).

Chapter 10

1. McDonald, Frank (1985), *The Destruction of Dublin*, Dublin : Gill and Macmillan, p. 1.
2. Policy 2.8.18 in the *1980 Dublin City Development Plan* aimed to restrict physical change in some areas of the centre city and to encourage it in others in the following terms

   "The Planning Authority will seek to correct the present imbalanced nature of office development as between the northern and southern parts of the Inner City. In general change and intensification of land use in the "Georgian" areas south of the Liffey shall be discouraged so that the character of the environment is conserved and the growth of traffic curtailed"

   This policy was translated into two particular development control standards. In the *1971 Dublin City Development Plan*, a maximum plot ratio of 1.0 had applied to areas zoned for residential and office use south of the Grand Canal, whereas a maximum of 2.0 applied in the rest of the residential and office zone. This standard was retained in the *1980 Plan* but, in addition, was strengthened by the provision that an office content of up to 100 per cent of the total floorspace could be allowed in areas to the north of the Liffey, whereas a maximum of 40 per cent only was permissible in areas south of the Liffey (pp. 92–93). Two particular examples of areas which failed to redevelop under these policies, Mountjoy Square and Gardiner Street, blossomed with the introduction of the 1986 Urban Renewal Act.
3. Urban Renewal Act, 1986 (Establishment of Custom House Docks Development Authority) Order, 1986 (SI 330 of 1986).
4. 1997 Dublin Docklands Development Authority Act, s. 56.
5. Custom House Docks Area, 1st extension, Urban Renewal (Amendment) Act, 1987 (Extension of Custom House Docks Area), Order, 1987 (SI 206 of 1987).

   Custom House Docks Area, 2nd extension, Urban Renewal (Amendment) Act, 1987 (Extension of Custom House Docks Area) Order, 1988 (SI 105 of 1988).

   Custom House Docks Area, 3rd extension, Urban Renewal (Amendment)Act, 1987 (Extension of Custom House Docks Area) Order, 1994 (SI 180 of 1994).
6. 1986 Urban Renewal Act, s. 12(6).
7. KPMG and Others (December 1996), *Study on the Urban Renewal Schemes*, Dublin : Stationery Office, p. viii.

8. *Ibid.*, p. 116.

9. *Report of the Dublin Docklands Area Task Force* (1996), Stationery Office, p. 36.

10. The *1996 Land Use and Condition Survey* was carried out by the Custom House Docks Development Authority itself. The *Inventory of the Architectural and Industrial Archaeological Heritage* was carried out by the School of Architecture, UCD. *The Socio–Economic and Employment Structure of the Dublin Docklands Area* was studied by the Economic and Social Research Institute.

11. 1997 Dublin Docklands Development Authority Act, s. 18(1)(a).

12. Consistency between the *Docklands Area Master Plan* and the *Dublin City Development Plan* is required by s. 24(5)(a) of the 1997 Act.

13. 1997 Act, s. 24(5)(b).

14. 1997 Act, s. 25.

15. See 1997 Act, sections 5,6 and 25.

16. Dublin Docklands Development Authority Act, 1997 (Extension of Custom House Docks Area) Order, 1998 (SI 344 of 1998).

17. Dublin Docklands Development Authority Act, 1997 (Transfer of Land) (No. 1) Order, 1999 (SI 37 of 1999).

18. The *Description of Temple Bar Area* contained in the First Schedule to the 1991 Temple Bar Area Renewal and Development Act delineated the extended area.

19. KPMG and Others, op. cit.

20. *Ibid.*, p. xii.

21. The contents of and procedure for making an Integrated Area Plan are contained in s. 7 of the 1998 Urban Renewal Act. The previous types of urban renewal schemes may be classified as follows:

1986	First Scheme was for the limited areas set out in the Fourth Schedule to the 1986 Finance Act
1988	Second Scheme extended the benefits of designation to provincial centres
1994	Third Scheme was more focussed, introducing the concepts of *Living over the Business and Enterprise areas.*
1998/99	Fourth Scheme was based on the Integrated Area Plans.
1999	Fifth Scheme is the Town Renewal Scheme launched in July 1999.

22. Peter Bacon & Associates and Others (April 1998), *An Economic Assessment of Recent House Price Developments*, Dublin : Stationery Office.

    Peter Bacon & Associates and Fergal McCabe (March 1999), *The Housing Market: an Economic Review and Assessment*, Dublin : Stationery Office.

23. The Architectural Heritage (National Inventory) and Historic Monuments (Miscellaneous Provisions) Act and the Local Government (Planning and Development) Act both completed their passage through the Oireachtas in Summer 1999.

24. Department of the Environment (July 1999), *Town Renewal Scheme Guidelines*, p. 3.

25. For the classification of urban renewal schemes, see note (21) above.

26. Department of Tourism and Trade (1995), *Pilot Tax Relief Scheme for Certain Resort Areas*. This brochure sets out the main features of the scheme and lists the areas designated.

Chapter 11

1. See Chapter 10, *Seaside Resorts, supra*, p. 61-2.

2. Brady Shipman Martin (1997), *Coastal Zone Management – a Draft Policy for Ireland*.

3. *Ibid.*, p. 67 and Fig. 6.1.

4. *Ibid.*, p. 68.

5. The 1997 Fisheries (Amendment) Act replaced the procedures under s. 15 of the 1959 Fisheries (Consolidation) Act and s. 54 of the 1980 Fisheries Act with a new system designed, in the words of the Minister at the second stage of the Bill in the Dail, 'to strike the necessary balance between the essential development needs of the aquaculture industry and the acknowledged and real concerns of other parties' (*Dáil Debates, 12 December 1996, col. 1153*). The procedures relating to appeals and their consideration by the Aquaculture Licenses Appeals Board are derived from the planning appeals procedure.

6. 1997 Fisheries (Amendment) Act, s. 61(c).

7. Aquaculture (Licence Application) Regulations, 1998, Article 10 (SI 236 of 1998).

8. Building Bye–Laws were made by eight authorities – Bray UDC, Dublin Corporation, Dublin County Council, Dun Laoghaire Corporation, Cork Corporation, Galway Corporation, Limerick Corporation and Naas UDC. For a description of their operation , see Galligan, E., *op. cit.*, p. 366.

9. 1990 Building Control Act, s. 3(2).

10. The commencement date, 1 June 1992, is given in Article 2 of the 1991 Building Regulations (SI 306 of 1991).

11. 1997 Building Regulations (SI 497 of 1997).

12. 1997 Building Control Regulations (SI 496 of 1997).

13. 1990 Building Control Act, s.2.

14. *Strengthening the Protection of the Architectural Heritage* (1996), Stationery Office, Dublin, p.104.

15. *Ibid.*, p. 105.

16. See Chapter 2, *Contents, supra,* p.6, for a discussion on the mandatory and optional elements in development plans.

17. 1999 Planning Act, s. 3.

18. The development of the Irish local authority system is briefly traced in Chapter 1, *Administrative Context, supra,* p.2. The larger or upper tier of local authorities consists of 29 county councils and 5 county borough corporations at present. For the local authorities at each level, see Appendix IV.

19. 1963 Planning Act, s. 19(2).

20. The definition of a derelict site contained in the 1990 Derelict Sites Act, s. 3, may be *summarised* as land or buildings which detract from the amenity, character or appearance of the neighbourhood because of the condition of the buildings, the appearance of the site or the presence of litter/waste thereon.

21. Environmental Protection Agency (1995), *Draft Guidelines on the Information to be Contained in Environmental Impact Statements,* Dublin: Environmental Publications, p. 11.

22. Council Directive of 27 June, 1985 (No. 85/337/EEC).

23. Appendix III contains a schedule of the Environmental Impact Assessment Regulations currently in force. For a discussion on the possible methods of implementing European Law in Ireland, see Scannell, Yvonne (1995), *Environmental and Planning Law,* Dublin : The Round Hall Press, pp.11–16.

24. *Meagher v Minister for Agriculture,* (1994) ILRM 1.

25. Council Directive of 3 March, 1997 (No. 97/11/EC).

26. Fry, John (1998), 'The Amended EIA Directive 1997', *Irish Planning and Environmental Law Journal,* vol. 5, no. 1, Dublin: Round Hall Sweet & Maxwell, p. 9.

27. 1989 EIA Regulations, Article 24.

28. 1994 Planning Regulations, Article 26(1).

29. 1999 Planning Regulations, Article 11, lists the categories of site which are to be considered environmentally sensitive.

30. 1989 EIA Regulations, Article 25 as amended by Article 6 of 1998 EIA Regulations.
31. Fry, J., *op. cit.*, p. 11.
32. 1999 Planning Regulations, Part II.
33. 1992 Environmental Protection Agency Act, s. 52.
34. Environmental Protection Agency (1994), *Integrated Pollution Control Licensing – A Guide to Implementation and Enforcement in Ireland*, Wexford : EPA, p.2.
35. 1992 Environmental Protection Agency Act, s. 98.
36. See Dobbyn, Ethna (1995), *The Implications of the Environmental Protection Agency for the Irish Planning System* (unpublished MRUP Thesis, UCD). The survey work for this thesis indicated an unexpected level of approval among planners for the two separate systems and there is general recognition that the degree of specialist knowledge required to evaluate certain processes justifies two parallel consent procedures.
37. Council Directive of 2 April 1979 (No. 79/409/EEC) (the 'Birds Directive') and Council Directive of 21 May 1992 (No. 92/43/EEC) (the 'Habitats Directive').
38. 1997 European Communities (Natural Habitats) Regulations (SI 94 of 1997).
39. Information obtained from Dúchas, the Heritage Service, on the number of sites notified by 31 August 1999.
40. 1997 Natural Habitats Regulations, Article 9 (SI 94 of 1997).

Chapter 12
1. The former Dublin County Council was divided into three separate administrative counties from 1 January 1994 under the 1993 Local Government (Dublin) Act.
2. The Tribunals of Inquiry (Evidence) Acts, 1921 and 1979, (No. 3) Order, 1997 made by the Minister for the Environment and Local Government on 4 November 1997, established the Tribunal of Inquiry into Certain Planning Matters and Payments.

Schedule of Planning Acts

1934–39 Town and Regional Planning Acts
1963 Local Government (Planning and Development) Act
1976 Local Government (Planning and Development) Act
- An Bord Pleanála established
- Planning Injunction (s.27)
- Withering of permissions
1982 Local Government (Planning and Development) Act
- Fees introduced
- Withering provisions amended
1983 Local Government (Planning and Development) Act
- Board reconstituted
1990 Local Government (Planning and Development) Act
- Compensation
1992 Local Government (Planning and Development) Act
- Appeals procedures changed
- Enforcement strengthened
1993 Local Government (Planning and Development) Act
- Development by State and Local Authorities
1998 Local Government (Planning and Development) Act
- Board membership
1999 Local Government (Planning and Development) Act
- Protection of the built heritage

Schedule of Local Government
(Planning and Development Regulations)

SI 86 of 1994

> Replaced and consolidated all previous Planning Regulations.

SI 69 of 1995

> Amendments in relation to IPC licences, Part X, height of extensions to dwellings and other types of exempted development, planning application procedures and requirements.

SI 75 of 1995

> Amendments to Part X making available for inspection documents in relation to appeals received after 10 April 1995.

SI 100 of 1996

> Amendment to A.13, lowering the threshold at which afforestation requires planning permission from 200 ha to 70 ha.

> (See also EC(EIA)(A) Regulations 1996 which made a corresponding change to the threshold at which afforestation requires EIA).

SI 78 of 1997

> Amended Second Schedule, creating exemptions for replacement masts and additional antennae for mobile telephony.

SI 121 of 1997

> Amendments in relation to circulation of development plans and planning applications (prescribed consultees) and to definition of classes for fees.

SI 261 of 1997

> Amendments consequential on the licensing system for waste disposal under the Waste Management Act, which is to be operated by the EPA.

SI 119 of 1998

> Revised fees payable to planning authorities and An Bord Pleanála from 1 May 1998.

SI 124 of 1998

> Removed exclusion of halting sites from the Part X procedure.

SI 128 of 1998

> Replaced SI 119 of 1998, revising fees payable to planning authorities and An Bord Pleanála from 1 May 1998 and 15 June 1998 respectively, thus enabling planning authorities to give notice of revised appeal fees when issuing decision.

SI 194 of 1998

> Removes change of use to supermarket over 3,000 m² from exempted status, to complement Policy Directive on Shopping (SI 193 of 1998).

SI 92 of 1999

> Amendments to procedures relating to scoping of Environmental Impact Statements, proposed development on environmentally sensitive sites and/or sites with transboundary implications.
>
> (see also EC (EIA) (A) Regulations 1999 which made related changes)

Schedule of Environmental Impact Assessment Regulations

European Communities (Environmental Impact Assessment) Regulation, 1989 (SI No. 349 of 1989).

European Communities (Environmental Impact Assessment) (Amendment) Regulations, 1994 (SI No. 84 of 1994).

European Communities (Environmental Impact Assessment) (Amendment) Regulations, 1996 (SI No. 101 of 1996).

European Communities (Environmental Impact Assessment) (Amendment) Regulations, 1998 (SI No. 351 of 1998).

European Communities (Environmental Impact Assessment) (Amendment) Regulations, 1999 (SI No. 93 of 1999).

Schedule of Local Authorities

(Note: Town Commissioners are not Planning Authorities)

County Councils

Carlow
Cavan
Clare
Cork
Donegal
Dun Laoghaire-Rathdown
  (formerly Dublin)
Fingal (formerly Dublin)
Galway
Kerry
Kildare
Kilkenny
Laois
Leitrim
Limerick
Longford
Louth
Mayo
Meath
Monaghan
Offaly
Roscommon
Sligo
South Dublin (formerly Dublin)
Tipperary (North Riding)
Tipperary (South Riding)
Waterford
Westmeath
Wexford
Wicklow

County Borough Corporations

Cork
Dublin
Galway
Limerick
Waterford

Borough Corporations

Clonmel
Drogheda
Kilkenny
Sligo
Wexford

Urban District Councils

Arklow
Athlone
Athy
Ballina
Ballinasloe
Birr
Bray
Buncrana
Bundoran
Carlow
Carrickmacross
Carrick-on-Suir
Cashel
Castlebar
Castleblayney
Cavan
Clonakilty
Clones
Cobh
Dundalk
Dungarvan
Ennis
Enniscorthy
Fermoy
Kells
Killarney
Kilrush
Kinsale
Letterkenny
Listowel

Longford
Macroom
Mallow
Midleton
Monaghan
Naas
Navan
Nenagh
New Ross
Skibbereen
Templemore
Thurles
Tipperary
Tralee
Trim
Tullamore
Westport
Wicklow
Youghal

Town Commissioners
Ardee, Co. Louth
Balbriggan, Co. Dublin
Ballybay, Co. Monaghan

Ballyshannon, Co. Donegal
Bandon, Co. Cork
Bantry, Co. Cork
Belturbet, Co. Cavan
Boyle, Co. Roscommon
Cootehill, Co. Cavan
Droichead Nua, Co. Kildare
Edenderry, Co. Offaly
Granard, Co. Longford
Greystones, Co. Wicklow
Gorey, Co. Wexford
Kilkee, Co. Clare
Leixlip, Co. Kildare
Lismore, Co. Waterford
Loughrea, Co. Galway
Mountmellick, Co. Laois
Muinebheag, Co. Carlow
Mullingar, Co. Westmeath
Passage West, Co. Cork
Portlaoise, Co. Laois
Shannon, Co. Clare
Tramore, Co. Waterford
Tuam, Co. Galway

Regional Authorities

Dublin Region
Dublin CBC
Dun Laoghaire-Rathdown
Fingal
South Dublin

Mid-East Region
Kildare
Meath
Wicklow

Mid-West Region
Clare
Limerick CBC and County
Tipperary (NR)

South-East Region
Carlow
Kilkenny
Tipperary (SR)
Waterford CBC and County
Wexford

South-West Region
Cork CBC and County
Kerry

The Southern and Eastern Regional Assembly will draw its members from the above Regional Authorities.

Border Region
Cavan
Donegal
Leitrim
Louth
Monaghan
Sligo

Midland Region
Offaly
Laois
Longford
Westmeath

West Region
Galway CBC and County
Mayo
Roscommon

The Border, Midland and Western Regional Assembly will draw its members from the above Regional Authorities.